With the flag to Ladysmith!

The march of Major General James Yule's brigade
from Dundee to Ladysmith
23 to 26 October 1899

Robin Smith

Assistance from too many people to thank individually – thank you all!

first published in South Africa by Robin W. Smith

Copyright 2009, 2025 © Robin W. Smith

ISBN: 978-1-917426-18-3

The right of Robin Smith to be identified as the author of this work has been asserted by the author in accordance with the UK Copyright, Designs and Patents Act 1988.

ll rights reserved. No part of this publication may be reproduced, stored in a retrieval system or transmitted, in any form or by any means without the prior written permission of the publisher, nor be otherwise circulated in any form of binding or cover other than that in which it is published and without a similar condition being imposed on the subsequent buyer.

Robin W. Smith

Military history researcher of Anglo Boer War sites.

**Major General James Yule's march
from Dundee to Ladysmith
22 to 26 October 1899**

Contents

Prologue	Major General Yule's march, a noteworthy feat of leadership.	5
Chapter 1	The difficulty of defending the Colony of Natal – 1895 to 1899.	6
Chapter 2	Commandant General Piet Joubert's Boer army – 25 September to 23 October 1899.	13
Chapter 3	Dundee – 11 to 23 October 1899.	20
Chapter4	The British and the Boers – 21 to 22 October 1899.	28
Chapter 5	The march begins – 22 to 25 October 1899.	34
Chapter 6	The slow Boer move southward – 24 to 26 October 1899.	39
Chapter 7	Across the Sundays River Valley – 25 to 26 October 1899.	44
Chapter 8	Safe in Ladysmith – 26 October and afterwards.	48
Orders of Battle	British and Boer armies.	51
Bibliography	Books and documents.	52
Index		52

Van Tonder's Pass – the British route down the Biggarsberg.

Prologue

Major General James Yule's march from Dundee to Ladysmith – 22nd to 26th October 1899

For three days and nights the British garrison of Dundee, the Glencoe Field Force, four thousand strong with eighteen guns and a long train of transport wagons, made their arduous way back to Ladysmith. Only three days before they started on their journey, they had succeeded in driving away a Boer force which had occupied Talana Hill overlooking the town from the east. A tactical victory for the British but won at the cost of five hundred casualties, of whom almost half were captured. Further Boer forces had arrived and were busily engaged in shelling their camp, the neat lines of white tents well within range of their big guns to which the outranged British artillery were unable to offer an effective reply.

The commanding officer of the British force, Major General Sir William Penn Symons, lay mortally wounded in the tent hospital. Telegraph communications with Ladysmith were still possible, via Greytown and Pietermaritzburg, as the direct line had been cut by the advancing Boers. Lieutenant General Sir George White in Ladysmith could offer no reinforcements. The railway line to Ladysmith had been cut. The road down the Glencoe Pass, the direct road link, was under the muzzles of the Boer guns.

The second-in-command, Brigadier General James Yule, was now in command, given the local rank of Major General, and there were insufficient experienced officers to command and organise the force. A decision had to be made to abandon the town of Dundee, with their wounded men and General Penn Symons, as well as large quantities of ammunition and stores. Were the Boers to pursue the retreating force, then a stand would have to be made to repel an attack or ambush. There were a number of places along the road where the Boers could wait in ambush, as the British well knew.

There was no alternative but to retreat down the only road still open – along the Helpmekaar road, down the escarpment via Van Tonder's Nek Pass. Then the route was across the wide valley of the Waschbank and Sundays Rivers, to enter Ladysmith from the east. It was nearly seventy miles to Ladysmith, over terrible roads and with two river crossings to be made. The weather was typical for the South African early summer – boiling hot during the daytime with frequent thunderstorms and torrential rain.

Not a single man was lost on the journey. A small number of wagons were perforce abandoned and some animals died in their traces, but – most valuable of all – their eighteen guns were added to the arsenal in Ladysmith. There can be no debate as to whether this welcome addition to the garrison of Ladysmith was key to enabling the British to hold the town for nigh on four months. The men from Dundee constituted a quarter of the force in Ladysmith. Truly, the orderly retreat was a remarkable exploit reflecting extremely well on the discipline of the men and the leadership of the officer corps.

It was another incident in the campaign and battles around Ladysmith in October 1899 which culminated in the town's encirclement by the armies of the Boer Republics of the Orange Free State and the Transvaal. Most of the men who made the march with Yule were besieged within the town and many indeed died there, principally of disease. Colonel Yule and his officers seem never to have received full recognition for his commitment and that of his officers to the success of this arduous task. While it may seem to have been a serious blunder to have placed them in Dundee in the first place, enabling their return to the defences of Ladysmith was leadership of a high order.

What follows is an account of their long march, told mostly by the men who took part in it, for many wrote of their experiences, in letters to newspapers and their families. Some kept diaries to tell of what so many of them regarded as a great adventure – perhaps not at the time, but certainly afterwards!

Chapter 1

The difficulty of defending the Colony of Natal: 1895 to 1899

"...most important events will have taken place and I shall be either a man or a mouse."
(Sir George White to his brother, 27th October 1899,
the day after the Glencoe Field Force arrived safely back in Ladysmith.)

The present boundaries of KwaZulu Natal are very different from those of the Colony of Natal in 1899. The districts of Utrecht and Vryheid were then part of the South African Republic of the Transvaal. From 1884 to 1888 they had been constituted as the New Republic with Lukas Meyer as its first President. The advantages of being part of the newly-rich Transvaal persuaded Meyer and his fellow office-holders to allow incorporation of their young state into the Boer state of the Transvaal on 20th July 1888. Britain had recognised the boundaries of the New Republic in 1886 and Zululand, for a time, became a British Colony until finally incorporated into the Colony of Natal in 1897. (Note 1)

With these districts to the east and the Orange Free State Republic to the west, northern Natal was a salient surrounded by Boer territory, hostile in the event of war. The first plans for the defence of Natal had been formulated in 1896 by the then commander of the British forces in Natal, Major General George Cox. Tensions were high in the aftermath of the abortive raid on Johannesburg by Cecil Rhodes's friend and confidante, Dr Leander Starr Jameson. (Note 2) The conclusion then was that northern Natal could not be defended. Only a detachment of Natal Mounted Police and a handful of Natal Colonial troops would be maintained in Newcastle. Boer forces could easily descend the Drakensberg passes from the Orange Free State and over the Buffalo River from the Transvaal to outflank any defenders north of the line of the Biggarsberg. As a consequence, the garrison in Ladysmith was strengthened in 1897 and there the troops were to be concentrated in the event of hostilities. (Note 3)

Lieutenant General Sir William Butler was appointed commander of British forces in South Africa following the sudden death of his predecessor, Lieutenant General Sir W.H. Goodenough. Butler arrived in Cape Town on 30th November 1898 and initially deputised for the High Commissioner, Sir Alfred Milner, while he was away in London on leave and for meetings with Joseph Chamberlain, the Colonial Secretary. Butler had been in South Africa twice before, in 1875 with Major General Garnet Wolseley and then in 1879 during the Anglo Zulu war. He was avowedly an admirer of the Boers. Soon after his arrival he made a speech at the South African Exhibition in Grahamstown saying "South Africa ... needs peace, progress and the development which is only possible through the union of many hearts and the labour of many hands." (Note 4)

In December 1898 Butler received a letter from the War Department which pressed him to formulate a scheme for the defence of the two colonies of the Cape and Natal. It furthermore recommended that advanced positions be occupied right up to the frontiers before the outbreak of hostilities. Butler journeyed to Natal in February 1899 and evolved a plan for its defence but he did not reply immediately to the War Office. His reasons were that this plan needed to be kept secret from possible enemies over the Drakensberg as well as "all my own people." He considered it most likely that, in the event of war, the Boers would invade northern Natal in force. The northern salient, which included Newcastle, Dundee and their coalfields, could not be defended by the force then at his disposal. The Ladysmith garrison should thus be used to entrench and fortify the pass in the Biggarsberg at Glencoe through which ran the railway line. The cavalry regiments and the Natal Police would be used as scouts to east and west of the railway, watching the passes over the Drakensberg and the drifts over the Buffalo River. Early news of Boer movements in superior numbers would allow the defenders to fall back to Ladysmith in the event of their being seriously threatened on either flank. A pull back to the line of the Tugela could also be entertained if needs be – with culverts and railway bridges destroyed – but retaining control of the railway line for supplies stores and ammunition. His reply went to the War Office only in June 1899. (Note 5)

Butler declined to ask for reinforcements for his small force in South Africa on the grounds that this might be provocation for the Boer Republics. Milner and Chamberlain were then engaged in a series of diplomatic manoeuvres with President Kruger and the South African Republic in the dispute over Uitlander rights. This ultimately led to the declaration of war by the Boer republic. Milner told Butler that he had hindered him in his designs on a number of occasions which left Butler no alternative but to resign his position as commander of British forces in South Africa. He left for England on 23rd August, 1899. (Note 6)

As early as May 1899 there were plans afoot to send a field force consisting of an army corps to South Africa and General Sir Redvers Buller was given command. Major General Sir William Penn Symons was sent from India to take command in Natal, arriving in July 1899 when war with the Boers was looking increasingly likely. On 8th September the British Cabinet authorized the sending of substantial reinforcements to South Africa – ten thousand men drawn from India, Egypt, Malta and Crete. Butler's successor was Lieutenant General Sir W.H.F. Forestier Walker who seems not to have become much involved in anything beyond the confines of the Cape Colony. The Secretary of State for War, Lord Lansdowne, considered that Penn Symons could hold the fort until Buller arrived but the Commander-in-Chief, Lord Wolseley, insisted that a more senior officer be sent to take command in Natal. The Quartermaster-General at the War Office was Lieutenant General Sir George White, V.C., an ex-commander of the British army in India and now sixty-four years old. He walked with a marked limp, legacy of a riding accident in India in 1897 and he seemed not suited for a field command as a result. His explanation to Wolseley that his leg was "good enough for anything except running away" seemed to satisfy Lansdowne and he was appointed to supersede Penn Symons, who he knew well from their time together in India and Burma. (Note 7)

White left Southampton on 16th September, 1899 with his two chosen staff officers, Colonel Ian Hamilton and Lieutenant Colonel Sir Henry Rawlinson both of whom were to take a prominent part in the Anglo Boer war and rise to high rank in the British army thereafter. White had not met in London with Buller who was to be his commanding officer in South Africa, although apparently there had been an exchange of letters – Buller had warned him not to go north of the Tugela River but White dismissed this as alarmist! Buller had had wide experience of South Africa, playing a prominent part in the Anglo Zulu war of 1879 in particular. He was concerned that there had been no strategy for the defence of Natal discussed with White, nor had White been issued any orders. Buller considered that "we have let things drift until we are in a very uncomfortable military position – if the Boers are bold … they have now the chance of inflicting a serious reverse upon us in Natal." (Note 8) White had no orders whatever to guide him – "rightly or wrongly, the War Office … had issued no instructions which could interfere with his entire freedom of action." (Note 9)

Arriving in Cape Town on 3rd October, White found things very different from what he had expected. When he left London, Lord Lansdowne was convinced that President Kruger was bluffing and would not go to war. On board ship the young Dutch-born Transvaal government secretary, Carl Sandberg, was equally certain that the Republic would not fight. Milner told White that the Boers had turned out in large numbers and were massed on the borders of the Colonies. An ultimatum was expected and hostilities might begin at any time. It was clear that the Orange Free State would make common cause with their counterparts across the Vaal by the terms of an alliance signed by Presidents Kruger and Steyn in 1897 which guaranteed Free State support in the event of a declaration of war by the Transvaal. For White, this was the worst possible scenario for the defence of Natal. The High Commissioner was convinced too that the Cape Afrikaners were "ripe for revolt". Worst of all was the news that Symons, acting on his own authority, had moved a brigade seventy miles north to Dundee, splitting the already meagre force in two. Forestier Walker was present at the meeting with Milner and White. At least agreement was reached that Natal was the likely point where a strong Boer incursion might be expected and that almost all the troops assembling there from overseas would be left for White.

Rather than wait a few days in Cape Town, White and his staff left immediately by train for East London and another ship so as to arrive the sooner in Durban. It was an interesting train journey with large numbers of armed Afrikaners gathered at the local stations who clearly sympathized with their compatriots in the Republics. The nature of the countryside was a surprise too although, being familiar with India, the arid Karoo must have reminded him of parts of that huge country. Train loads of refugees from Johannesburg passed in the opposite direction, many of them women and children. He seems to have realised just how difficult his task was going to be for he wrote to his wife on board the SS *Scot* that "we should have 20,000 more troops in South Africa than we have … the Cabinet have only themselves to thank if they have to reconquer South Africa from the sea." (Note 10)

General Sir Redvers Buller had not been permitted to organise the force which he was to command and could only select certain of the staff who were to accompany him. For his chief of staff he wanted Major General Archibald Hunter, then in command of British forces in Quetta on the North West frontier of India on the border with Afghanistan (nowadays Pakistan and still troublesome). Hunter was the hero of Omdurman when Kitchener's Egyptian army defeated the Khalifa Abdullahi, revenged General Gordon's murder and recaptured the Sudan. Quetta was a plum posting for a junior Major General but he spent only a few months in the post before he was notified to proceed to South Africa. He arrived in Durban on 6th October, a few days before Sir George White and more than three weeks before Buller was due in the country. In Pietermaritzburg he made acquaintance once again with the Governor of Natal, Sir Walter Hely-Hutchinson. Hunter had been best man at Sir Walter's wedding when they had both been serving in Barbados in 1879. His orders for now were to attach himself to Sir George White's staff which must have annoyed Ian Hamilton, three years his senior but still only a Colonel. (Note 11)

White arrived on 7th October, spent two days in Durban and could only wait for Penn Symons to appear. On Monday, 9th October 1899 White and his staff travelled to Pietermaritzburg. That evening they met with the Governor and Hunter. Symons and White's military secretary, Major Beauchamp Duff were also present. Buller had issued the warning – do not go north of the Tugela. Rawlinson, perhaps White's ablest staff officer, described the situation:

> This distribution of the military forces in Natal, to my mind and also to Sir George's, is an impossible one. The Boers are known to have some 15,000 to 20,000 men on the frontier, and all told we have not 10,000 in Natal. Yet these are split up, half at Glencoe and half at Ladysmith, both of which are, in my opinion, much too far forward to secure the defence of the Colony.
>
> It is my conviction that if Natal is to be defended successfully with the forces that we have available, against an enemy greatly superior in numbers, and armed with modern weapons, the only thing to do is to hold the line of the Tugela and give up Dundee and Ladysmith altogether. But I understand that the Governor will not hear of our even leaving Dundee. He is afraid of the moral effect of a retirement on the Boers in the Cape Colony, and on the natives. The native problem is one with which we are faced wherever we go, and it is a difficult one, but we should not allow it to force us into false positions. It seems to me that the effect on the natives will be much greater if we are driven back than if we fall back. If we don't go back to the Tugela we shall be roughly handled.
>
> I don't much like the tone amongst our fellows out here. Symons is brim full of confidence, and all the rest follow him. They talk as if the war were over, now a brigade is coming from India, and speak of a British brigade being able to take on in five times in Boers, which is silly rot. (Note 12)

White came to the meeting with the intention of withdrawing the brigade now at Dundee and Glencoe at least back to Ladysmith. They were militarily in a dangerous position, liable to be cut off and impossible to reinforce. Symons was in favour of continuing to occupy the two positions and was contemptuous of the fighting qualities of the Boers. Hunter, although he had been in South Africa only a few days and had no knowledge of the country, was consulted and seems to have given the opinion that, under the circumstances, the troops should stay where they were. White was seriously disquieted by the Governor's attitude which Hely-Hutchinson put into writing in his report of the meeting to the Colonial Secretary:

> Now that we are there, withdrawal would, in my opinion, involve grave political results, loyalists would be disgusted and discouraged; the results as regards the Dutch would be grave, many, if not most, would very likely rise, believing us to be afraid, and the evil might very likely spread to the Dutch in the Cape Colony; and the effect on our natives, of whom there were 750,000 in Natal and Zululand, might be disastrous. They as yet believe in our power – they look to us – but if we withdraw from Glencoe they will look on it in the light of a defeat, and I could not answer for what they, or at all events a large proportion of them, might do." (Note 13)

After some discussion, White reluctantly agreed to maintain the status quo. He was, after all, new to South Africa and the opinion of the Governor would have carried some weight. He had once described Penn Symons as "the most competent man in India to command an infantry division" so the opinion of his Natal commander would not have been taken lightly. The coal mines around Dundee and Newcastle and the possible loss of their output, seem not to have entered the discussions. (Note 14)

While the defence of Natal was being discussed, another meeting was taking place in Pretoria. The State Secretary of the Transvaal, Francis Reitz, and a former President of the Orange Free State until ill-health forced his retirement, called at 5 p.m. to see the British Resident, Mr William Conyngham Greene. He handed over an ultimatum demanding of the British Government that they reply within forty-eight hours. The joint ultimatum had been decided upon by the two republics by the end of September but President Steyn of the Orange Free State still hesitated. The ultimatum, which had begun as a short document, at Steyn's insistence became much longer, but the terms were the same. The British government was required to give the Transvaal government an assurance that:

- All points of difference would be submitted to arbitration by a neutral power.

- British troops on the borders of the republic would be instantly withdrawn.
- British reinforcements which had arrived since 1st June would be withdrawn from South Africa.
- All British troops which are now on the high seas will not be landed at any port in South Africa.

Unless the British government complied with these demands within forty-eight hours, the Transvaal would "with great regret be compelled to regard the action as a formal declaration of war." The British government was not prepared to enter into any discussion concerning this document and as White and his staff travelled by Natal Government Railway to Ladysmith the ultimatum ran out. Britain was at war with the Republics. Crucial to the defence of Natal, President Steyn on 11th October declared the support of the Orange Free State for "our kith and kin" in the Transvaal. (Note 15)

The delay of almost two weeks in drafting the ultimatum document allowed the British reinforcements, the first of whom landed on the 8th October, to entrain and travel to Ladysmith. By the time White arrived in Ladysmith they had all arrived and settled in, with the exception of the 1st Battalion of the Gloucestershire Regiment who arrived on 15th October and some of the 5th Dragoon Guards who arrived just before Ladysmith was encircled by the Boers. The immediate task was an inspection of the town's defences. Ladysmith is surrounded by hills and its defence would be difficult although White's stated intention was to attack any Boer forces that came near enough. On 13th October most of his force was sent out nine miles to the west after some patrols of the Natal Carbineers reported that the Free Staters had descended into Natal. Nothing was found and the Dublin Fusiliers, brought down from Dundee in the morning were returned in the evening. (Note 16)

White seems to have been feeling more comfortable about his situation and the division of his forces by the 15th October when the Gloucesters arrived in Ladysmith. More cavalry were due in a few days and so it was decided to send the 1st Battalion of the Royal Irish Rifles to Dundee. On the morning of 15th October Lieutenant Colonel Rawlinson and the Ladysmith Brigade Major, Captain John Vallentin joined some of the officers of the Royal Irish Rifles for a journey on the armoured train to Glencoe and then on to Dundee, on a branch line and a further three miles away. The rest of the regiment arrived the following day, 16th October. This seems curious in view of White's serious reservation about the wisdom of splitting his force when he knew that he was shortly to face a Boer army that would considerably outnumber the British force. (Note 17)

On his return to Ladysmith that night, Rawlinson was closely questioned by his commander about the state of the defences at Dundee. Rawlinson responded that there were no defences as such but, most importantly, the water supply could not be protected as its source was a large cistern on Impati mountain to the north of the town. (Note 18) This was in direct violation of White's instructions to Symons since it was conditional upon these requirements that he had consented to retain the force at Dundee. Nevertheless it was three days before he telegraphed to Penn Symons that, unless he could assure White of his compliance, he was to immediately evacuate his forces, supplies and the civilian inhabitants back to Ladysmith. The railway line between the two towns was vulnerable to attack and elements of Commandant General Piet Joubert's Transvaal army, even though advancing with special caution, were closing in. To send all the available rolling stock to Dundee would have been foolhardy and Penn Symons telegraphed that "We can and must stay here" to which White could only reply that "I fully support you. Difficulties and disadvantages of other course have decided me to support your views." (Note 19)

All that remained for Major General Sir William Penn Symons and the British Brigade in Dundee was to defend the town against the Boers advancing on them from the north and east. By ignoring Buller's warnings, White and Symons soon found themselves in difficulties. It seems likely that White, and perhaps even Symons, may have been aware of Butler's plan for the defence of the Colony. As an alternative to a total withdrawal to Ladysmith and beyond, to the line of the Tugela, it merited serious consideration but clearly was ignored.

One more thing escaped White's notice and that was the unhealthy state of public health in Ladysmith. Butler had moved almost half the garrison to the more healthy surroundings of Nottingham Road, some forty miles to the south, early in 1899. (Note 20) White's neglect of this aspect was to cost him dearly when once the town was surrounded by the forces of his enemies. Surely though, at this time he was not anticipating being shut up in the town for nigh on four months. From 2nd November until the siege was lifted on 28th February 1900, the ravages of enteric fever cost him many more casualties than Boer bullets.

Notes on sources:
1. John Laband *Zulus and the War* explains how the New Republic came to be formed from land given to Boers from the Transvaal who assisted Dinizulu caCetshwayo, the claimant to the Zulu thone, in defeating his rival Zibhebhu. See Laband's chapter in John Gooch *The Boer War* pp110-111.
2. "The Jameson Raid was the real declaration of war in the Great Anglo-Boer conflict…And that is so in spite of the four years that followed…[the] aggressors consolidated their alliance…the defenders on the other hand silently and grimly prepared for the inevitable." Jan Smuts in 1906.
3. Amery *Times History* Vol II pp 102-103 and Maurice *History of the War in South Africa* Vol 1 pp35-38.
4. The conclusion of the speech is quoted in Butler's *An Autobiography* p398.
5. Butler *An Autobiography* pp418-421.
6. Butler *An Autobiography* p454 and Amery *Times History* Vol II p102.
7. Durand *The Life of Field-Marshal Sir George White* Vol II p7.
8. From a letter, Buller to Lord Lansdowne, 9th September 1899.
9. Durand *The Life of Field-Marshal Sir George White* Vol II p18.
10. Letter to Lady White dated 6th October 1899 quoted in Pakenham, The Boer War p99. Durand *The Life of Field-Marshal Sir George White* p26 quotes from a letter of the same date which has an altogether more optimistic tone!
11. Hunter *Kitchener's Sword Arm* p118.
12. Maurice *Soldier, Artist, Sportsman* p45.
13. Natal governor, Sir Walter Hely-Hutchinson, quoted in Maurice, *The War in South Africa* Vol 1 p47.
14. Durand *The Life of Field-Marshal Sir George White* Vol II p19.
15. Smith *The Origins of the South African War* pp379-381.
16. Amery *Times History* Vol II p145. A number of diaries and accounts by members of the Natal Colonial regiments give details of these movements.
17. Churcher *With the Irish Fusiliers* pp14-15 tells of how the 1st RIR moved to Dundee on 15th and 16th October. Neither the *Times History* nor *The War in South Africa* (the Official History) mentions this.
18. The War in South Africa merely states "an officer of the Headquarters staff"; from Churcher *With the Irish Fusiliers* p14 it is clear that the officer is Rawlinson.
19. Maurice *History of the War in South Africa* Vol 1 p127.
20. Butler *An Autobiography* p416.

Northern Natal in 1899

From Maurice "History of the War in South Africa 1899 – 1902" – the Official History

Lieutenant Colonel
Sir Albert Hime, KCMG
Prime Minister of Natal 1899

Right Honourable
Harry Escombe
Prime Minister of Natal 1897

British Officials in South Africa, 1899:
Top left: Sir Alfred Milner – High Commissioner for South Africa and Governor of the Cape.
Above right: Mr William Conyngham-Greene – British Resident in Pretoria.
Left: Sir Walter Hely-Hutchinson – Governor of Natal.

Major General Sir William Penn Symons   Colonel James Yule   Lieutenant General Sir George White   Lieutenant General Sir William Butler

The defenders of the Colony of Natal

Chapter 2

Commandant General Piet Joubert's Boer Army
25 September to 23 October 1899

"The Boers, 18,000 strong with fourteen guns, crossed the frontier of Natal
at daybreak in three widely separated columns ..."
(German Official Account of the War in South Africa)

A huge Boer army assembled at Sandspruit to await the declaration of war. Denys Reitz, the 17-year-old son of Francis Reitz, was there too having travelled by train from Pretoria with his fellow soldiers and their horses. It had taken three days to get there but in spite of this "they were full of ardour". This must have been on 2nd October as he says that they were there for ten days. He described the scene: (Note 1)

> We saw the stream of fresh contingents arriving daily by rail, or riding in from the adjacent countryside, and watched with never-ending interest the long columns of shaggy men on shaggy horses passing by. At the end of the week there must have been nearly 15,000 horsemen collected here, ready to invade Natal, and we told ourselves that nothing could stop us reaching the sea. On 10th of October a great parade was held in honour of President Kruger's birthday. We mustered then what must have been the largest body of mounted men ever seen in South Africa. It was magnificent to see commando after commando file past the Commandant General, each man brandishing hat or rifle according to his individual idea of a military salute. After the march-past we formed in mass, and galloped cheering up the slope, where Piet Joubert sat his horse beneath an embroidered banner. He addressed us from the saddle ... saying that an ultimatum had been sent to the British, giving them twenty-four hours in which to withdraw their troops from the borders of the Republic, failing which there was to be war. The excitement was immense. The great throng stood in its stirrups and shouted itself hoarse.

Reitz was prone to exaggerate due no doubt to the excitement of the occasion, for actually present at the front were some 6,700 men from eight commandos, together with 2,700 foreign volunteers, German, Dutch, Irish and a few Italians. A little further away were three commandos from the districts of Utrecht, Vryheid and Piet Retief, amounting to a further 1,700 while over to the west were the men from the Orange Free State covering the various passes over the Drakensberg leading down into Natal – their numbers amounted to a further 6,040. All in all, the Boers had rapidly mobilized and put into the field no less than 17,400 men, armed with modern magazine rifles and most of them on their own horses. (Note 2)

The march to Sandspruit and then on to Volksrust was not an orderly affair and J.F. Naudé tells of his march with the Boksburg commando: (translation from the Afrikaans)

> So, to Volksrust! There was no question of a regular procession. The commands were well separated and moved one behind the other, but if Commandant A allowed his commando to go too slowly, commandant B went right past, and so also with the field-cornetcies. A burger from Germiston talks suddenly with one from Pretoria and one from Pretoria rides alongside one from Heidelberg. It becomes really mixed up – those on horses in front, then the mules pulling the carts and right at the back the ox wagons. Such a state of irregularity and disorder was not to the liking of those who preferred to see things happening in an orderly fashion. (Note 3)

Rain and mist delayed their advance into Natal but three columns crossed the border on 12th October. Reitz and the Pretoria commando were part of the force under the command of General D.J.E. "Maroela" Erasmus – so called because in the recent campaign against the chief Magoeba in the northern Transvaal, according to Reitz, "he was said to have directed operations from behind a maroela tree." They advanced through the mountains into the district of Utrecht and suffered two nights of torrential rain and cold winds from the Drakensberg. On the 14th October they made to cross the Buffalo River into Natal at Wools Drift:

> General Maroola, with a quick eye to the occasion, faced around and made a speech telling us that Natal was a heritage filched from our forefathers, which must now be recovered from the usurper. Amid enthusiastic cries we began to ford the stream. It took nearly an hour for all to cross, and during this time the cheering and singing of the "Volkslied" was continuous, and we rode into the smiling land of Natal full of hope and courage. (Note 4)

The first Boers over the border were General Jan Kock's men. They crossed over at midday on 11th October, even before the expiry of the ultimatum. They camped for the night at the Ingogo River and captured an employee of the Natal Government who was engaged in repairing the bridge. After taking his scotch cart as booty, the man was escorted in to Newcastle to join his wife and family. Colonel Adolf Schiel who commanded the German Corps complained that the Johannesburg commando invaded Natal like the Huns. A deserted shop at the foot of the Drakensberg was broken into and plundered. General Kock complained to Schiel about the breakdown of discipline and sent a message to Joubert to recall Field Cornet Pienaar and put him up before a court martial. Pienaar in turn complained to Joubert about Kock. Joubert's fatherly reaction was to request them all to work sincerely together since "unity was vital to uphold the independence of the country." (Note 5)

Looting was a huge problem for Joubert, not only with the Johannesburgers. The very first commando to open the toll-gate and enter Natal were the Hollander Corps under Commandant J.P. la G. Lombard. With much singing and merriment they advanced to the village of Charlestown where they helped themselves to "one pair of hats" from an Indian's store which had "already been broken into." (Note 6) In Newcastle, which the commandos reached on 14th October, the shops and many of the houses were laid waste. J.F. Naudé and his colleagues from Germiston were disgusted at the action of their Field Cornet Derckse. Instead of restraining the plundering, Derckse seems to have encouraged it. (translation from the Afrikaans)

> To make matters worse, the Field Cornet dismounted in the town and gave a free hand to those who had not restrained themselves. We sought them out and immediately expressed our disapproval in the strongest language as otherwise everyone would have had to bear the blame. When the calf had already drowned, an order was given that nothing must be damaged but it was already midday before the commando left town. (Note 7)

This provoked a strong reaction and Naudé and the Germiston men demanded that they be formed into a separate unit and to be permitted to elect their own Field Cornet, Oom Naas van Wyk. (Note 8) Joubert had already, on 7th October, issued instructions to all Boer officers that there was to be no robbery and plundering of "private, individual homes or farms where no enemy was sited" and that anything taken out of necessity for the use of the commandos must only be done with a receipt promising payment by the government of the South African Republic. He backed this up with a proclamation on 17th October to the inhabitants of Natal wherein he pledged that the Boers would "wage war in the most civilized and humanitarian manner under the leadership of the almighty God in heaven, and will seek and drive for peace. May it come quickly!" (translation from the Dutch) Things went so far that the State Attorney, Jan Smuts, was sent to Natal to attend to legal proceedings against the transgressors. Joubert had already requested that a number of officials be sent to assist with the administrative work of the invasion in order that he might concentrate on the campaign. (Note 9)

A council of war was called by Joubert in Newcastle on 16th October. The reason was primarily to comply with the commando law of the South African Republic which required that any plan of campaign must first be agreed to by a council of war composed of all Commandants, Field Cornets, Assistant Field Cornets and Head Artillery officers present. (Note 10) Steps needed also to be taken to restore some order to the army. Decisions were taken to attack the British force at Dundee as Joubert's prime objective. Erasmus was to move with the main force to Dannhauser Station while Kock's men were to advance from Newcastle over the Biggarsberg to cut the rail link between Dundee and Ladysmith. Kock should also get in touch with the Free Staters who should by now have descended down the Drakensberg passes to the vicinity of and to the west of Ladysmith. Once Dundee was isolated then Erasmus was to attack from the north and Lucas Meyer from the east. Erasmus was also to ensure that the road to Ladysmith was not to be usable as an escape route by the British. It was known that the hills surrounding the town were not occupied and fortified. Once the railway and telegraph lines were cut the enemy should be dealt with before the Boer army could move on to Ladysmith and the much larger garrison there.

Wynand Malan, then an ordinary burger but who later rose to be a General during the guerilla phase of the war in the Cape Colony in 1901-02, tells an amusing (but improbable) story of how he and his uncle chased a patrol of five Natal Mounted Police through Dannhauser. Erasmus was unwilling to advance until the countryside had been scouted but Malan volunteered. Field Cornet Esterhuizen and twelve men had accompanied Malan but Esterhuizen took fright when the five policemen were spotted and refused to proceed further saying, "The ridges are full of English". The cautious advance of the Boers through the undefended territory of northern Natal frustrated many of the burgers, like Reitz, but time had to be given to allow the stragglers to close up and the wagons lagged far behind. (Note 11)

Lucas Meyer had moved the Vrede and Utrecht commandos to a laager behind the Doringberg, not far from De Jager's Drift, then in the Transvaal and within ten miles of Dundee. Meyer's men had patrolled the area and Commandant Louis Botha and some Vryheid Boers crossed into Natal and captured five men of the Natal Mounted Police who apparently were unaware of the outbreak of war. Botha patrolled right up to within sight of Dundee and camped there for the night on 14th October, according to one account. The Middelburg and Wakkerstroom commandos arrived to support Meyer on 12th October but the Krugersdorp and Bethel commandos, who had travelled over poor roads in thick, deep mud, arrived in an exhausted state and with their animals in poor condition. General Schalk Burger with 250 men and three guns was expected from Bell's Kop on the border with Swaziland but he could not possibly arrive until after 19th October. (Note 12)

Meyer called a council of war, as the law demanded, on 18th October and a majority vote required that they advance towards Dundee even though they were not yet prepared for battle. That the Commandant General was pressing Meyer hard to get moving certainly was a factor in their decision. They moved up to and over Vant's Drift on the evening of 19th October. Couriers were sent to get in touch with Erasmus who at that time was at the foot of the Imbabane hills, still about six miles away from Dundee. Erasmus had advanced painfully slowly and much of his force was still around Dannhauser Station. Naudé and his friends had been joined by other burgers from Germiston when the word spread that they had formed a separate unit, Field Cornet Derckse clearly not a popular man. He tells of their wait at the station: (translated from the Afrikaans)

> The sun had already begun to sink towards the horizon and the drizzle had started to fall even harder when we rode towards Dannhauser station in order to get a little shelter for the night for ourselves and our animals. When we got near and the burghers saw that there was scarcely cover for even half of them, they simply rushed the place. There were lots of harsh words uttered in order to occupy and keep a little space. The empty houses and stables were occupied in an instant, and as our wagons were behind us and everyone had just a blanket and a jacket, so we spent the night on the station squashed together. It was the night of 19th October, the eve of the battle that we were to undertake together at Dundee.
>
> At two o'clock we awaken so as to occupy the hills on the northwest of Dundee and attack the enemy there as well as in Dundee. Two o'clock came; three, four o'clock went by and still no order was given to leave. It got light, the dawn broke, everyone was ready, and still no order.
>
> But listen! What is that? No, there it is again. One boom after the other. Those are cannons roaring, they attack, our burgers fight!
>
> Everyone runs to their horses, throws the saddle onto their back and stands ready to mount, full of fire and flame to take part. Why do we linger? Must we lie here while our fellow burgers are shot dead? Where is the commandant? Why does he not let us get going? Such questions and many other words besides are heard from all sides. Some of the more impatient ones who can no longer be compelled to remain, climb on their horses but are immediately ordered by Derckse not to go one yard further before the commandant has given the order.
>
> Here the burgers sit and are prevented by their officers from helping their brothers because the commandant has given them no orders to do so. And why has commandant Weilbach not given the desired orders? Because General Erasmus has perhaps given no order? And why has no order been given by General Erasmus? Or has it perhaps been done? (Note 13)

Erasmus had indeed gone forward and some of the Boers had climbed Impati, the high mountain overlooking Dundee from the north west. Reitz was with them. After they had spent the whole day on 19th October halted in sight of that flat-topped mountain, at sunset they were given orders for another night march. His account describes the advance up the steep slopes:

> General Maroola, with the 1,500 men of whom we of the Pretoria Commando formed part, was to occupy the mountain overlooking the enemy's camp at Dundee, while the other forces were to complete the pincers on the flanks and rear. There was much excitement at the prospect of fighting, and even the heavy rain that had set in after we started did not depress our spirits. The night was black, and our route seemed to lie chiefly over an open mud-bound plain, varied at times by more broken country in the passage of which there was a great deal of confusion and intermingling between the different commandos, but for all that, steady progress was made, and towards dawn Maroola succeeded in disentangling his commando from

> the other columns. Soon the frequent lightning revealed the steep side of the mountain ... this was the mountain from the top of which it was said that one could look down on the English encampments on the other side ... When we reached the wide plateau we found it deserted. ... as it was pitch dark, and the rain was coming down in torrents, we waited shivering in the cold for the coming of daybreak. (Note 14)

On 19th October General Erasmus and Colonel S.P.E. Trichardt went to discuss a coordinated attack on Dundee. They met "halfway between the two laagers" but there seems to have been no record kept of this meeting between the officers of the two parts of the army. Apparently, General Lucas Meyer sent a "certain Breijtenbach" to the meeting. It seems to have been agreed that Meyer would form the left wing with the commandos of Vryheid and Utrecht, Erasmus would be in the centre with the Pretoria commando and Commandant Hans Grobler with the Ermelo commando and Trichardt with the Transvaal artillery would be on the right. Commandant J.D. Weilbach with the Heidelbergers was still at Dannhauser Station but not yet ordered to move forward to the ridges overlooking Glencoe to block any British attempt to escape along the best road to Ladysmith. (Note 15)

On the morning of 19th October the railway line was cut at Elandslaagte station. General Jan Kock's men had descended the Biggarsberg in such a disorderly mob that Colonel Adolf Schiel saw fit to complain in writing to Kock. What Kock did about it is not known for two scouting patrols sent forward from Commandant Ben Viljoen's Johannesburg commando had captured a train laden with good things for the officer's mess at Dundee as it steamed into the station early that day. An earlier train, on its way northwards, had stopped for shunting, but escaped in a shower of rifle bullets. The driver had had the presence of mind to put on steam when he saw mounted men around the station. Messages were sent by Field Cornet Potgieter to Schiel for assistance. Schiel took his commando forward and arrived at the station. The other Field Cornet at Elandslaagte, Pienaar sent his report to Viljoen who sent a courier instructing him to "destroy the rail line and come directly back." Viljoen was concerned that an advance to Elandslaagte had not been authorised by the council of war two days previously. In addition, at Elandslaagte they would be far ahead of the rest of the army and not in touch with other commandos on left and right. Kock, on the other hand, sent a message to Schiel that he should: "Hold the trains under all circumstances; I am following with my whole force." Kock advanced to Elandslaagte, established his laager in some low hills behind the station, sent a message that Colonel Trichardt should move on Waschbank, the next station up the line, to protect his position, and awaited developments. (Note 16)

The Commandant General had been concerned about the possibility of a British invasion of Transvaal territory through Zululand but Meyer had established that there were only two hundred British troops in Eshowe, so this was unlikely. Another of Joubert's fears was of an invasion from the sea through Tongaland which is why Schalk Burger's strong commando with three guns was placed on the Swaziland border. Once this possibility was eliminated, Burger was ordered to join Meyer at Doringberg but he was so far away that he would not be able to arrive in time for an attack on Dundee. Joubert was also rightly concerned that the strong British force in Dundee would cross into the Transvaal, only a few miles away, at one of the three nearby drifts over the Buffalo River. He was worried as well that the there would be an attack on Erasmus before Meyer had moved into position. Erasmus had encountered a strong British patrol north of Hattingspruit but had declined to engage them. Another force left Dundee by train at 3 a.m. on 19th October and went to Navigation Collieries to bring back eight tons of mealies which could not be just left for the Boers. (Note 17)

Meyer sent a message that "our movement today (19th October) up to the Buffalo River is enough to keep Dundee in their camp". (translated from the Dutch) As the sun went down on 19th October, Meyer and the commandos of Utrecht and Wakkerstroom with some men of the Krugersdorp, Vryheid and Ermelo commandos headed out of their camp behind the Doringberg. They crossed the Buffalo at De Jager's Drift at about 9 p.m. and emerged onto the veld east of Dundee. At a crossroads where the tracks from Landman's and Vant's Drift met, the Boer scouts encountered Lieutenant C.T.W. Grimshaw's picket of the Dublin Fusiliers. Shots were exchanged, the Dublin's horses took fright and Grimshaw's men retired back towards Dundee. The scouts were on top of Talana Hill well before daybreak and Meyer with his two commandos, two Creusot 75mm guns and a 37.5mm Vickers-Maxim were close behind: (translation from the Afrikaans)

> "Say good morning to the old English, captain," a few burgers standing next to the Krupps (sic) excitedly encouraged General Meyer. "Yes, yes!" ordered Meyer as if he had suddenly come to a decision, "let it go, old son!" At 5.50 a.m., according to the official report of Sir George White, the cannon's morning greeting roared

out over the valley and the bombardment of the British camp commenced. (Note 18)

Once the initial shock had worn off, for the British were taken somewhat by surprise, their frontal attack on the hill later in the morning sent Meyer's commandos in retreat back the way they had come taking with them the bodies of thirty of their comrades and leaving behind their three guns.

Joubert must have communicated his fears of a British attack on Erasmus to his general and counseled caution. In spite of a tacit agreement to cooperate with Meyer in an attack on Dundee, Erasmus stood by and did nothing. While the British artillery, three batteries or eighteen guns in all, pounded the Boers on the top of Talana and the infantry stormed up the slope, Erasmus made no move. Reitz's experience confirms this:

> When it grew light the rain ceased, but a mist enshrouded the mountain-top. ... When Maroola was asked for orders he merely stood glowering into the fog without reply. ...we knew that the English lines were immediately below us ... and we expected to be led down the face of the mountain to the attack. But General Maroola and his brother made no sign, and when President Kruger's son Caspar, who was serving with us as a private, and who for once in his life showed a little spirit, went up and implored them to march us to the enemy, Maroola curtly ordered him off.
>
> We could see nothing, but heavy fighting had started close by, for the roar of the guns increased and at times we heard the rattle of small arms and Maxims. None of the fire, however, was directed at us and so far as we were concerned nothing happened, and we fretted at the thought of standing passively by when others were striking the first blow of the War. After perhaps an hour the sound died down, indicating, although we did not know it at the time, that the English had driven the Vryheid men from Talana Hill with heavy losses. Towards midday the weather cleared somewhat, and while it still continued misty, patches of sunshine began to splash the plain behind us, across which we had approached the mountain overnight. (Note 19)

This first Boer attack had been disastrous. Meyer had attacked and occupied Talana Hill and Lennox Hill further south but had received no additional support from the thousands of Boers on Impati and kicking their heels at Dannhauser Station. The weather had been misty and to attack down the mountain with such poor visibility would have been unwise. Clearly it was impossible for the several forces to communicate with one another. However, their strategy and tactics had not been properly decided beforehand and General Lucas Meyer in particular seems to have thought that he could easily overwhelm the British garrison of four thousand regular soldiers.

What none of the Boer generals had yet realised, as the afternoon wore on, was that the day's proceedings had been just as disastrous for the British.

The Boer commanders:
Left: Commandant General Piet Joubert.
Above: Generals Lucas Meyer, Louis Botha (not yet a General), "Maroela" Erasmus.

With the Flag to Ladysmith

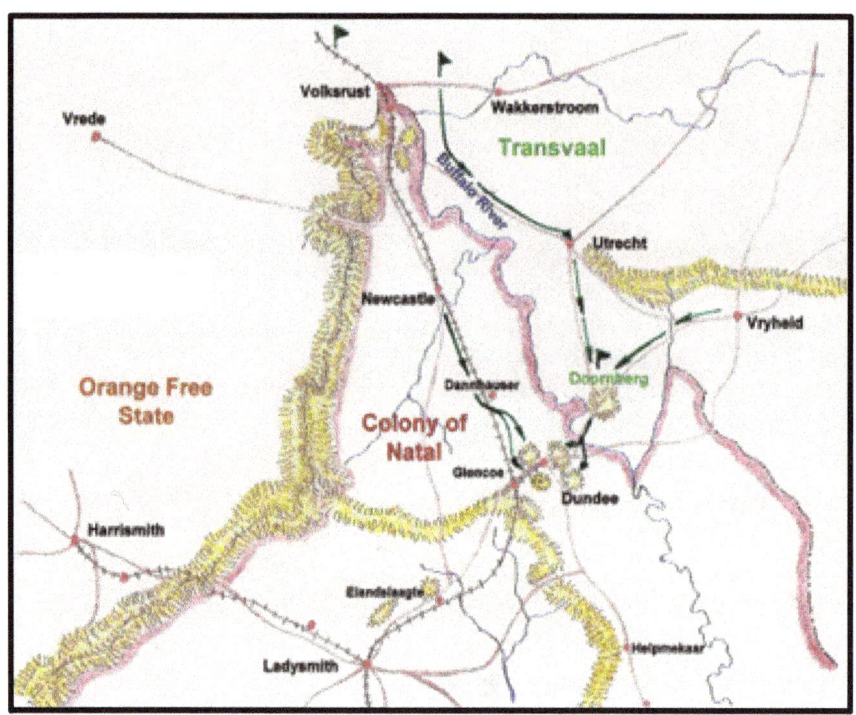

The Boer advance into the Colony of Natal:

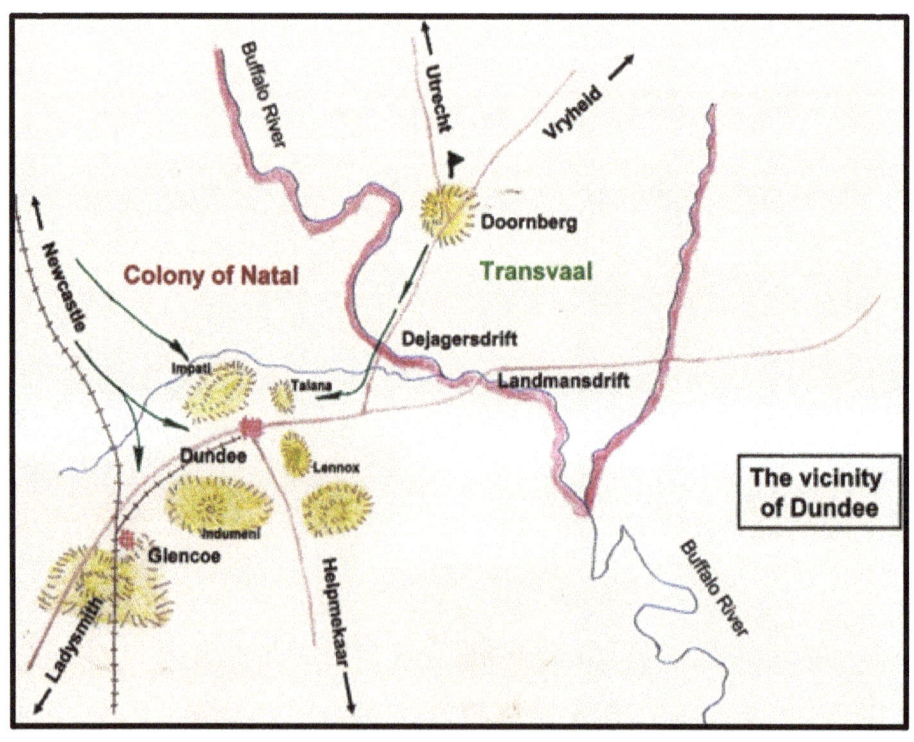

Notes on sources:
1. Reitz *Commando* pp21 and 23.
2. Breytenbach *Die Geskiedenis van die Tweede Vryheidsoorlog* Vol I pp 160-161 has tables showing the numbers given in the returns of the commandants to the Commandant General on 11th October 1899, pp160-161.
3. J.F. Naudé *Veg en Vlug* p23.
4. Reitz *Commando* p26.
5. Breytenbach *Die Geskiedenis van die Tweede Vryheidsoorlog* Vol I p182.
6. Breytenbach *Die Geskiedenis van die Tweede Vryheidsoorlog* Vol I p181.
7. J.F. Naudé *Veg en Vlug* p28.
8. J.F. Naudé *Veg en Vlug* p28.
9. Breytenbach *Die Geskiedenis van die Tweede Vryheidsoorlog* Vol I pp183 and 185.
10. Breytenbach *Die Geskiedenis van die Tweede Vryheidsoorlog* Vol I p167.
11. Pieterse *Oorlogsavonture van Genl. Wynand Malan* pp12-13. Written in the 1940' from interviews with Malan when memories might have faded somewhat.
12. Breytenbach *Die Geskiedenis van die Tweede Vryheidsoorlog* Vol I p188.
13. J.F. Naudé *Veg en Vlug* p33-34.
14. Reitz *Commando* pp27-28.
15. Breytenbach *Die Geskiedenis van die Tweede Vryheidsoorlog* Vol I pp189-190.
16. Breytenbach *Die Geskiedenis van die Tweede Vryheidsoorlog* Vol I pp191-194. A patrol of the 18th Hussars was close enough to the Boer army to see "about 2,000 of them…were seen by our scouts moving down the Biggarsberg Neck." Burnett *The 18th Hussars in South Africa* p6. In the next chapter is more about the train that escaped to Dundee.
17. Burnett *The 18th Hussars in South Africa* p6: "On Thursday, the 19th, we sent three companies of the Dublin Fusiliers to the Navigation Collieries to bring in some 1,000 bags of mealies which had been stacked there…"
18. This little anecdote appears in Preller *Talana* pp192-202 and is quoted in Breytenbach, *Die Geskiedenis van die Tweede Vryheidsoorlog* Vol I p217.
19. Reitz *Commando* p28.

Chapter 3

Dundee
11 to 23 October 1899

*"Whatever the estimate formed of the fighting qualities of the Boers –
and no one rated it lower than Sir William Penn Symons, who commanded the forces in Natal – …"*
(Amery, *The Times History of the war in South Africa Vol II* p103)

Major General Sir William Penn Symons was well known to his commander, Lieutenant General Sir George White, from their time in India and Burma together. White considered Symons to be exceptionally able and had described him as "the most competent man in India to command an infantry division." Symons, on hearing that White was to take command in Natal had written to him:

> The situation is as critical as it can be, and I am ready to move troops into their positions to do their best to protect Natal. I respect our maybe enemy for his love of independence, for his power of mobility, and for his marksmanship. I think also he has behaved fairly well in previous wars. His rule however is abominably bad and corrupt.

White's biographer, Sir Mortimer Durand said that, "it was a comfort to White to feel that he had on the spot already, awaiting his arrival, so brave and capable a soldier, and one who so thoroughly recognised the importance of the issue." (Note 1)

Long before Symons's arrival in Natal early in July 1899, there had been concern by the government of Natal as to whether the defence arrangements were adequate, particularly in respect of northern Natal and the coal mines around Newcastle and Dundee. The Prime Minister of Natal, Sir Albert Hime, was a former Colonel of the Natal Volunteers and may have had a more realistic outlook than Symons as to the intentions of the Boer republics and the military capability of their armies. Sir Alfred Milner was contacted directly by the Governor of Natal and, without consulting Butler, his military commander, Milner assured Hime and his Cabinet that Natal would be defended by "the whole force of the Empire." Pressed further by Hime as to the provisions made for a surprise attack, Hely-Hutchinson responded that Symons did not consider that, with the forces than at his disposal, Newcastle and the northern apex of Natal could even be defended. This was something of a surprise to the Prime Minister!

With the Boers able to put 40,000 men in the field in a matter of days, British reinforcements in the form of a fully-equipped Army corps would take thirteen weeks to be landed six thousand miles from home in South Africa. With this in mind and war with the Boer republics now well-nigh a certainty, the British government, on 8th September, decided to send 10,000 men from India and the Mediterranean which would "raise the garrison of South Africa without delay to a strength sufficient to repel any aggression on the part of the Boers." With these troops at war strength and a week closer to South Africa than England, they would arrive in early October. The question being however, would the Boers wait before opening hostilities? It was fortuitous that President Steyn's hesitation about the wording of the Boer ultimatum and his reluctance to call out his commandos played into the hands of the British. Most of these reinforcements had arrived by the outbreak of war but the British were still heavily outnumbered and would be for several months hence.

Even knowing all this, Symons was completely confident. Dundee was in a bowl, completely surrounded by hills through the gaps in which ran the roads and the railway. Impati, to the north west is a huge tableland which commands the whole northern half of the valley in which Dundee lay. The road to Hattingspruit, Dannhauser and Newcastle ran over its shoulder. A ridge running south west to Glencoe overlooked the railway line and road running through the pass over the Biggarsberg. On the east are two hills, Talana, and to its south, Lennox. The road to the drifts over the Buffalo River ran through Smith's Nek between these two. By seizing these hills, the Boers could make it extremely difficult and dangerous for the British to get through these passes, whether for attack or escape. Symons was not able to occupy and fortify these dominant features and indeed made no effort to do so.

Amery, writing in *The Times History* described Symons's situation like this:

> These considerations (the lie of the land, just described) do not seem to have weighed at all with the impetuous officer commanding at Dundee. His idea was to lie in wait in the valley till the Boers on one side or other came within striking distance and then to attack them whenever or wherever they appeared. If he formulated any more detailed plan to stem the flood of invasion, he was careful to conceal it from his subordinates. His open assertion was that he had no plans and intended to be guided

by circumstances, and he lost no opportunity of expressing his conviction that no number of Boers could venture deliberately to attack a whole brigade of British troops. (Note 2)

In the mess of the 60th Rifles the officers wore their scarlet and green dress uniforms. There were guest nights in the regimental mess and there was no shortage of whisky and soda. There was no problem with the morale of the garrison. Penn Symons was well liked even though his ideas on strategy were not thought to be attuned to the circumstances. His infantry battalions were now well-trained although he had complained to White in July that some of them had not been worked hard for a number of years. Without doubt their commander had licked them into shape but his officers were astonished at his reliance on old-fashioned close order. It was just as if they were still in India.

Penn Symons and his well-disciplined troops were appreciated by the folk in Dundee too. The Reverend Gerard Bailey, the young Anglican minister of St James's Church had a busy day on Sunday 15th October. He held a service at the camp at 9.30 a.m:

> There was a very full parade at the camp service. The band of the King's Royal Rifles played the hymns. General Penn Symons was present and I remember he came up to me before the service and said he hoped the camp service did not clash with my parish duties.
>
> He was always bright, affable and genial, and easily accessible, and on this account was very popular with the townspeople. The whole service was very impressive. A friend of mine photographed the parade, and I hope the picture has survived. (Note 3)

Most astonishing of all is this account by an officer of the 18th Hussars about a ride by more than fifty of them on Tuesday 17th October. The Boers then were well south of Newcastle and some Natal Mounted Police had been captured by Boer patrols on the Natal bank of the Buffalo River three days previously:

> In the orders of Monday evening appeared a notice that the general intended to ride up Impati Mountain the next day, and all officers who cared to accompany him would be welcome. This mountain lies to the west of Dundee and overlooked our camp. It is about 6,000 feet high, has a broad flat top nearly a mile long, devoid of trees, and on its south-eastern side its slopes are precipitous. From the summit one gets a fine extensive view of the country, the various hills and gorges, the open plains extending to the Buffalo, intersected here and there by winding spruits, and far away in the distance one catches a glimpse of the mountains in Zululand, near to which the Prince Imperial met his death. All the officers who could be spared from duty collected near the General's tent at 9 a.m. that Tuesday morning. We must have numbered at least fifty, and, now I come to think of it, we ran no small risk, for had the Boers, whom we knew to be no great distance off, taken it into their heads to attack us that morning, whilst the officer commanding and most of his Staff and other officers were engaged in toiling up the slopes of Impati, things would have been mighty unpleasant for the Glencoe Field Force. Or supposing this unsuspecting party of excursionists, personally conducted by the General, had been taken prisoners, what a beginning to the war! Such a catastrophe was, no doubt, hardly likely, but not an impossibility. The half company of Mounted Infantry, who escorted us, were our only safeguard. On the way we stopped to examine the waterworks which supplied Dundee with water, then a long circuitous path led us to the summit. The last part had been very steep, and a severe pull up for the ponies, but, once the top was reached, our climb was well rewarded by the glorious panorama which was spread before us. We got a magnificent birds-eye view of the surrounding country. Just below us lay the tents of the camp, and beyond them the small town of Dundee. On Impati we found a signaling post situated, a few men of the 18th Hussars under Captain Davey. We heard that, shortly before our arrival, a suspicious-looking individual had been detected watching the camp through field glasses, but that, before they could get up to him, he had mounted his pony, scrambled down the side of the mountain at the risk of his neck, and made for a farmhouse which we could plainly see below. The man, they said, was still inside the farmhouse, as they had never ceased watching it, and his pony was still tied up under a tree outside. Captain Lonsdale, of the Dublin Fusiliers, who was in command of the Mounted Infantry which had accompanied us up, asked the General whether he might ride down and try to capture this spy. The General having no objection, Lonsdale sallied forth with a few of his men. I sat down to await events, but as he had a long ride before him and I had to get back to camp, I did not wait for the dénoument, but I heard afterwards that the farm had been drawn blank, the bird had flown away, and the house had been stripped of every stick of furniture." (Note 4)

Major A.J. Murray, the chief British Intelligence officer was not as complacent as his General. Scouts along the Buffalo River reported that Boer commandos at De Jager's Drift were making ready to move. It was put to Symons that cavalry detachments should be placed at the intersection of the roads from Vant's and Landman's drifts, a few miles outside Dundee. But Symons insisted that he wanted his cavalry to be "fresh for action" and told his officers that "I have informed Sir George White that I feel perfectly safe, and I am dead against retreating. He has wired back wishing us 'good luck.'"

Shortly afterwards, the morning of 19th October, came the news that the Boers had occupied Elandslaagte Station and captured a supply train on its way to Dundee. Now cut off from Dundee, White was convinced that the Boers intended an attack on the British garrison there. A certain Simpson had given a letter to the British Intelligence stating that the "Boers intend attacking Dundee from Helpmekaar, Dannhauser and Glencoe sides." This information was substantially correct and Symons received a message from Colonel E.A. Altham, British Intelligence in Pietermaritzburg at 2.40 p.m. which read:

> No. 39 Magistrate Dundee wires today, begins: Three commandos intend attacking Dundee tonight; one from the west, 1000 under Viljoen, another from the North, 5000, under Erasmus, another, 9000, under Lucas Meyer, from East. From reliable source repeated. (Note 5)

Symons was also in possession of information from Bantu scouts and spies that the Boers intended an attack and was prepared for such an onslaught on 19th October. However, he failed to move the British camp, which was in a gently sloping field just outside Dundee, to defendable fortifications in the surrounding hills. He knew that the camp could easily be bombarded by Boer artillery should they occupy the hills overlooking the town.

That day the Dublin Fusiliers had collected the thousand sacks of mealies at Dannhauser station, as related in Chapter 2. Later in the day, a party of fifty King's Royal Rifles was sent by train to Waschbank station. There they collected a number of trucks that had been left at the station by the train driver who had escaped from Field Cornet Pienaar's men at Elandslaagte the previous night. The driver had left them there in order to make quicker time to Dundee but the KRR men collected them and returned to Dundee without mishap. Major D.W. Churcher of the Royal Irish Fusiliers had walked into town that morning, bought a pair of gumboots and found that he could have a bath in the hotel. They gave him a "great big bath full of hot water for which they charged nothing, so I stayed and had tea." Then things started happening:

> While two or three of us were sitting in the verandah having tea, Faulkner, a correspondent turned up, having just come through with a train from Ladysmith; he was much excited and told us that they had been fired on by a party of Boers at the small station of Elands Laagte, just this side of Ladysmith, but had managed to scrape through unhurt, although it must have been a pretty close shave, and Faulkner showed us his revolver which he had tried to fire off, but it miss-fired. We went down to see the train, and sure enough the engine was spattered with bullets, and the driver was holding forth to an admiring crowd. It appeared they were shunting at the time, and had to leave half the train behind which the Boers collared. While we were there a company of the 60th turned up and set off with an engine and two trucks to try and bring the abandoned half of the train in. (Note 6)

Commandant Weilbach with his Heidelberg commando and Commandant Derckse with the Boksburg men should surely have by now been along the ridge overlooking Glencoe. Had they been in position they would certainly have prevented both sallies from Dundee. No order to do so was given even though Joubert had now established his headquarters in Dannhauser.

Meyer advanced across the Buffalo River at De Jager's Drift and ran into Lieutenant Cecil Grimshaw's picket where the tracks from De Jager's and Landman's Drifts met. Grimshaw tells what happened to him in an account that he wrote some time afterwards:

> In the afternoon of the 19th of Oct (Thursday) orders came in to us at 3.30 to furnish a picquet of 12 men on the Landsman's Drift road in the vicinity of the cross roads leading to Landsman's Drift & Barrts Drift. (Vant's Drift)
>
> I was sent for picquet and left camp at 4.30 p.m., having given the men their dinners and had the horses fed, going round by a circuitous route to my post.
>
> Here I arrived just at dusk and I don't know why, but somehow, I thought that something was going to happen, so I fell the men in & warned them to be very careful and alert and that if anyone advanced without answering their challenge after the third time to shoot them, unless they had very good reasons for thinking they could not be heard. After this little oration I sent out my patrols warning them that I was going to move the position of my picquet

after dark. This I did, leaving a sentry (double) on the road. About 7 p.m. it began to pour and we were all pretty well soaked through in an hour. Just about 8 p.m., my sentry on the road challenged someone who did not answer, he challenged twice, but still no answer, I rushed over to see what it was and luckily recognized Mr Robinson, one of our intelligence officers with another man and 2 bantu scouts. It was very well I did as the next moment he would have been shot as the sentry had loaded and I had drawn my revolver ready to shoot.

I asked him why he had not answered and he said he had passed my scouts and told them who he was and thought that was alright.

He had never been given any "countersign" or anything, and if I had not happened to have known him from meeting him sometime before at polo it might have been a very serious thing. However from him I learned that a force of Boers, about 200 strong, had moved across Mulamgeni Mountain about 6 miles to my front, moving in a southerly direction. This seemed to be all he knew about them, but it was quite enough for me, as I knew that there was a commando behind the Doorneberg, so it kept me on the "gin-some". All went quite smoothly and at 1.30 a.m. I relieved my patrol, or rather sent out the relief.

Just after the old relief had come in and settled down, I heard horses' hoofs clattering on the road some distance out in front, as if they had galloped off the veldt across the road and on to the veldt again. I turned to my sentry and asked him if he had heard it, and he said "yes! It sounded like horses".

About 10 minutes after this I heard my patrol out in front challenging and getting no answer. They challenged three times. Then they fired and I knew the show had begun as their fire was returned at once. As soon as my patrol was clear I opened fire and kept it up for a bit on the mounted figures of men in front, as soon as the enemy's bullets began coming near the picquet all the ponies who were linked went off like a streak of lightening knocking down their guard and cleared.

The Boers came on, I should think there were about 20 of them and I retired slowly back up the hill towards the neck keeping off the road, which I maintained saved us, as we had heard the bullets pinging on the road to our left.

After the second retirement I found one of my men lying on the ground and asked him what was the matter. He said he was shot and I said where, he said in the arm. I tried to get him to rise and walk as we were being fired on heavily and had to retire, but he said, "Oh Christ, I am shot let me die." This shows you what a trouble he was. So I had to lift him up and got him back behind the firing line and then opened fire again on the Boers, who seemed to be increasing in number and I thought trying to get round us to cut us off. Here I suddenly spied a lot of our horses up against the line and I left the men in position with Sergeant Guilfoyle who was a rotter, but I would not trust any of the men to catch the horses and I went round got behind them and fortunately found my mare was still with them. I called to her and she knew me at once, and let me come up to her, and as the others were all tied to her I captured the lot of them. Four had gone altogether, then I returned the men on them and again tried to get Pte. Brenman who was wounded up on one & send him in, but he refused. First of all I forgot to say I sent my sergeant in on one of the horses as far as he could go to take a message to the effect that we had been attacked and were retiring on the neck, that the Boers appeared to be advancing in large numbers. (Note 7)

Grimshaw's sergeant arrived in the camp at 3 a.m. but Symons considered that this was only a small scale raid by the Boers and merely ordered two companies of Dublin Fusiliers to join Grimshaw at the Sandspruit, to which Grimshaw and his men had retired. A picket of the 18th Hussars had also been fired on when they went up Talana Hill to investigate some figures that had been seen on the summit. At 5 a.m. the camp stood to arms as usual and Headquarters assured all commanding officers that all was clear twenty minutes later. Half an hour after that, the first shell from the Boers on Talana landed in the western part of the town and the Boer bombardment began. The British had many more guns than the Boers and they soon silenced the Boer guns.

Symons's response now was to drive his enemy away by means of a frontal attack up the western slope of Talana. Very few of his soldiers had ever seen action. They were armed with Lee Metford and Lee Enfield magazine rifles – formidable modern weapons that at effective range could send a bullet through a nine-inch brick wall. The Boers had Mauser rifles with almost identical power and range. No European army had ever before faced concentrated fire from the magazine rifle although Talana was not the first demonstration of this awesome power – in the campaign in the Sudan the year before, British magazine rifles had decimated the Dervish hordes. (Note 8)

There was no lack of courage on the part of the infantry but the men were unwilling to brave the storm of fire coming from the Boers on the summit. None of their adversaries were visible and the smokeless ammunition did not reveal their whereabouts. The commander of the infantry brigade was Brigadier General James Yule, promoted from commanding officer of the Devonshire Regiment and sent to Dundee from India. Lieutenant Colonel F.R.C. Carleton of the Royal Irish Fusiliers sent his men to line a stone wall at the foot of the hill and the assault stalled. The 60th Rifles had been bested by the Boers at Majuba eighteen years previously and this was an opportunity to wipe away the stain on their honour. Colonel Robert Gunning urged them forward but the invisible riflemen on Talana forced them to find shelter in ditches and behind the stone walls of Smith's farm. (Note 9)

It was just after 9 a.m. when Symons arrived to enquire what had caused the delay in the attack. There must be no delay – Meyer's men must be pushed off the hill before Erasmus attacked from the west. His mounted orderly carried a lance with a red pennant which was the most inviting of targets for the Boer marksmen. One of their bullets struck home as he strode through an opening in the stone wall. He was hit in the abdomen, even managing to walk back to his horse. Then, out of sight of the troops, he was carried back to the camp hospital by his Indian stretcher bearers. The wound was mortal and he died three days later as the Boers entered the town.

Gunning was killed urging his men to attack up the steep rocky slope just short of the summit but the attack was driven home. (Note 10) This is the Reverend Gerard Bailey's rather dramatic description of the steep climb:

> Smith's Hill must be climbed before anyone can realise the immensely difficult and dangerous task the infantry had before them. It was a task which only could have been accomplished by the most fearless pluck. It is marvellous, considering the good marksmanship of the Boer, that we did not lose more lives. There was no stealing up the hill by some path unknown to the enemy, it was straight up the face of it that our men went. And then it is when one climbs the hill that one fully sees how fearfully galling must have been the cross-fire from the hill on the right. As you stand at the wall where the infantry lay so long, the other hill overlooks you, and I think it must have been from the cross-fire we suffered most. The enemy had proved themselves no mean foe. It was their first encounter with shell fire, and ours was so hot that it is no wonder that they were disconcerted from the very first. (Note 11)

Just after midday it was all over. The Boers of General Meyer's force had been sent back the way they had come. They left three of their guns behind but the British were unable to remove them. Five hundred British soldiers were casualties. Among them was part of a squadron of 18th Hussars who wandered westwards behind Impati under the leadership of their commander, Colonel B.D. Möller. They took refuge in Adelaide farm, were surrounded by Colonel Trichardt's artillerymen and some of the Pretoria commando and forced to surrender when the Boers brought up a Maxim Nordenfeldt gun. Among them were mounted infantrymen from the Royal Dublin Fusiliers, including Lieutenant Cecil Grimshaw. (Note 12)

Erasmus on Impati made no move to attack from the west, his only contribution being the capture of the Hussars. Meyer apparently tried repeatedly to contact Erasmus by heliograph but it is likely that the thick mist that day interfered with the transmissions. Meyer expressed his disappointment to Joubert that the men under Erasmus did not appear on the battlefield, although an arrangement had been made concerning the day and the hour of his attack. He complained in similar vein to his wife saying, "Erasmus did not appear with the result that the enemy almost had us surrounded." (translated from the Dutch) (Note 13) There seems to be little explanation for this lack of action from Erasmus although the weather was misty with incessant rain and from the top of Impati they could see nothing of Dundee and the action that was taking place.

The most likely reason is that Erasmus was waiting for the Boer's secret weapon to arrive, the 6-inch Creusot Long Tom gun. The War Office's own secret handbook, Military Notes on the Dutch Republics said it was out of the question to remove such ordnance from the forts overlooking Pretoria and utilise it in the field. Even more ridiculous was the idea that such a gun could be taken to the top of a mountain. On Saturday 21st October, the day after the battle, the gun arrived on the summit of Impati. (Note 14)

Major Churcher had had the misfortune, if indeed it was, of being left behind with 'G' company of the RIF as camp guards. He and his men had been on picquet on the edge of the camp and were "absolutely soaked to the skin and perished with cold." The regiment came back to camp at about 5.30 p.m. and as Churcher had been the only officer who had not been away from camp he was ordered to take half a company and picquet under the hill where the battle had taken place. This is his description of what was clearly a pretty miserable night:

It was dark before we reached the place, and the rain was pouring in torrents, so we stumbled about in a vague way till I thought we were about right, when I stopped on the near side of a barbed wire fence, which I thought would stop a rush. We had each brought a waterproof sheet, but there was little or nothing to be done except walk up and down and try and keep warm; we were wet through long before this. Nothing happened during the night – the most miserable I ever spent, as we had been out in the rain since early morning, and nothing to eat except a chunk of corned beef and a biscuit. Luckily I had a small flask of whiskey, which warmed me up nicely. (Note 15)

Command of the Glencoe Field Force now devolved upon Brigadier General James Yule. Symons's totally misplaced confidence that the Boers would never dare to attack a British brigade had placed Yule in an unenviable position. A number of staff officers were killed and seriously wounded so that he needed to create a new staff. For a while, so far as Yule knew, Colonel Möller and his cavalry had just disappeared but confirmation that they had been captured soon arrived. Decisions needed to be made about defending the camp and town. Yule had more realistic views about the strategic position of Dundee and was reluctant to retreat – however events would now conspire to force him to do so. (Note 16)

Notes on sources:

1. Durand *The Life of Field-Marshal Sir George White* Vol II p20.
2. Amery *The Times History of the war in South Africa* Vol II pp150-151.
3. Gerard Bailey *Seven months under Boer rule* p19. The photo-graph taken by his friend of the parade, regrettably, did not survive.
4. Burnett *The 18th Hussars in South Africa* pp8-9.
5. Breytenbach, *Die Geskiedenis van die Tweede Vryheidsoorlog* Vol I p212.
6. Churcher *With the Irish Fusiliers from Alexandria to Natal* pp17-18.
7. This is an extract from an unpublished diary by Lieutenant C.T.W. Grimshaw, My experiences in the Boer War, which graphically describes this sequence of events.
8. Asher *Khartoum – the Ultimate Imperial Adventure* p344 has a concise description of the power of magazine rifles. There is also one of the many accounts of the destruction of the Dervish empire by the British and Egyptian armies under Major General Sir Herbert Kitchener (as he then was) who became the commander in South Africa at the end of 1900.
9. During the nineteenth century, and before the rank of Brigadier was established in 1928, a local or temporary rank of Brigadier General was granted typically to a Colonel when commanding a brigade consisting of two or more regiments. James Yule at Dundee, a substantive Colonel, commanded the infantry brigade with such a local rank.
10. The spot where Colonel Bobby Gunning was killed is known with some accuracy and there is a marker at the place on Talana Hill. He was in the firing line and may have been one of several victims of friendly fire from the British artillery. See letter from Captain A.R.M. Stuart Wortley in the archive of the Royal Green Jackets museum in Winchester.
11. Gerard Bailey *Seven months under Boer rule* p29.
12. Breytenbach, *Die Geskiedenis van die Tweede Vryheidsoorlog* Vol I p232 quotes two sources. White's report of 2nd November: "Three of their guns were left dismounted on Talana Hill, but there was no opportunity of bringing them away." Meyer, on the other had told a journalist in an interview that "none of our guns were either captured or disabled."
13. Breytenbach, *Die Geskiedenis van die Tweede Vryheidsoorlog* Vol I pp232-233 quotes these two letters but does not hazard any reason for Erasmus's behaviour.
14. Lionel Crook *Artillery of the Anglo-Boer War 1899-1902* p190.
15. Churcher *With the Irish Fusiliers from Alexandria to Natal* pp19-20.
16. Yule's actions during the night and the morning after the battle would seem to indicate that he acted decisively to make the best of his invidious position. This may be at variance with a number of accounts which describe Yule as uncertain and wavering.

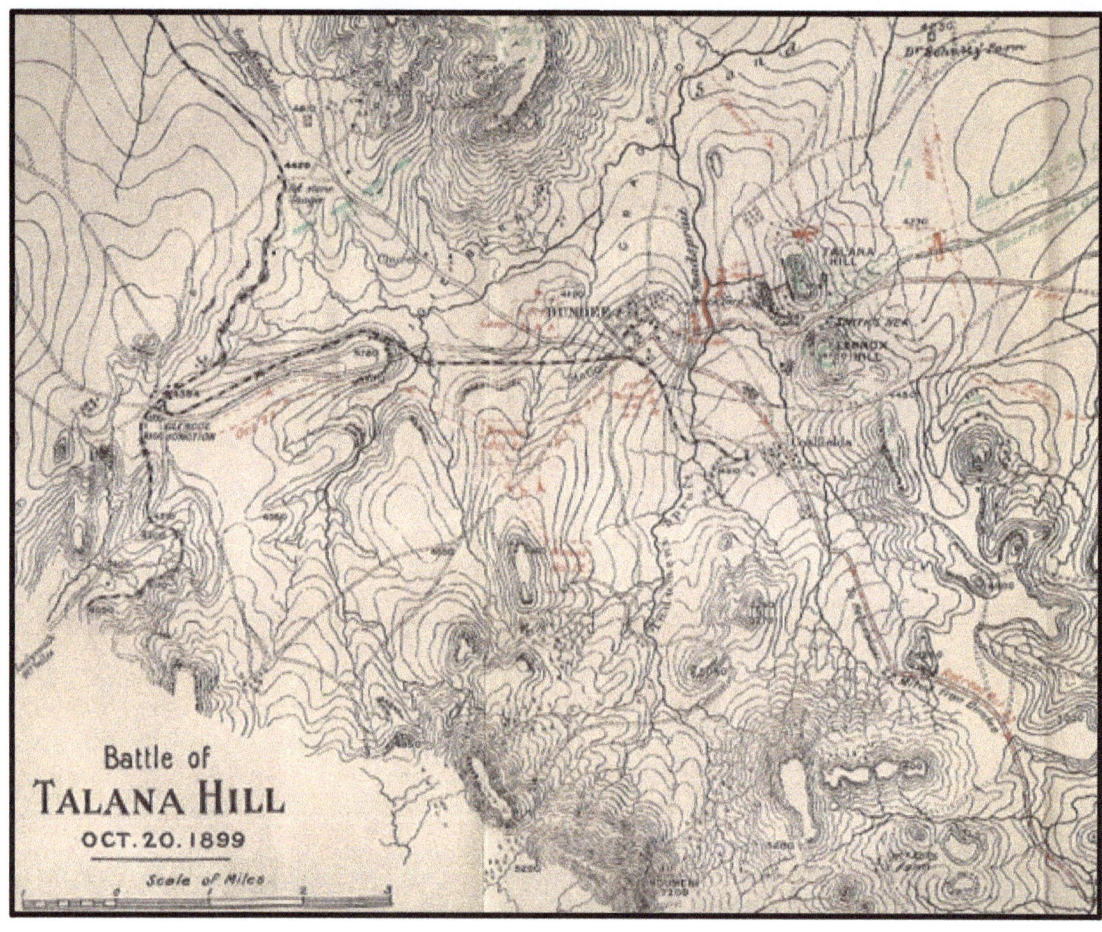

From Amery *The Times History of the War in South Africa*.

The battle of Talana
from *Die Geskiedenis van die Tweede Vryheidsoorlog 1899-1902* by J.H. Breytenbach

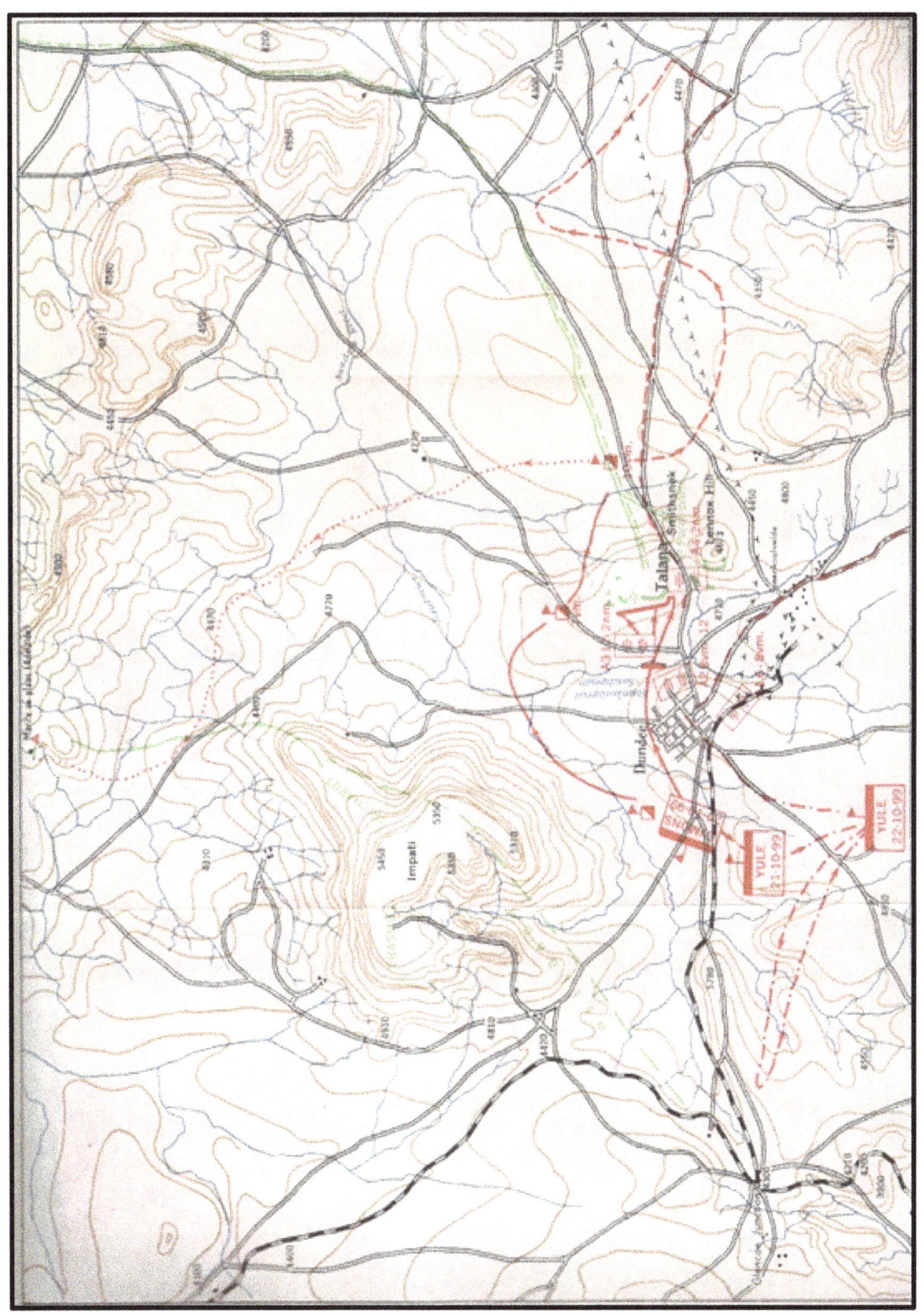

Chapter 4

The British and the Boers
21 to 22 October 1899

"You should never have let one single man of the entire army escape that day."
(A remark made by General J.H. de la Rey to Louis Botha after the war.)

Brigadier General James Yule was 52 years of age and an experienced soldier. Almost certainly the very first thing that he did on Saturday morning, 21st October, was to telegraph White in Ladysmith asking for reinforcements, food and ammunition. The reply came at 1.30 p.m. and was to the effect that no troops could be sent and that Yule should attempt to fall back on Ladysmith. White would help further when they got nearer. This response came from a staff officer, likely Hunter or Rawlinson, as White was occupied at Elandslaagte. Yule was reluctant to abandon his wounded, and especially the mortally wounded Symons, as well as the large accumulation of ammunition and supplies that had been stockpiled in the camp. The town was tactically indefensible and the camp was well within range of the Boer guns on Impati which were expected to open up at any time. An 18th Hussars' patrol had reported that morning that the Boers were bringing five guns up the northern slopes of Impati and another Hussar squadron had seen a big gun (likely the Creusot Long Tom) being detrained at Hattingspruit station. (Note 1)

Yule gave orders for the camp to be moved to a new site further away from Impati and for entrenchments to be dug. This move had hardly been started when the Boer guns opened fire. Shells fell on the old camp and, to the surprise of the British, on the new entrenchments as well, which were at a range of 7,000 yards. There was some damage to the tents and baggage and some casualties, one of them being Lieutenant W.M.J. Hannah of the Leicestershire Regiment who had volunteered to come to South Africa "for the fun of it." The British guns did not have sufficient range to silence those of the Boers and so the camp had perforce to be moved a second time. It was another uncomfortable night for the Royal Irish Fusiliers and Churcher describes what happened:

> About 2 a.m. we got the order to retire on to a low range of hills still further away, and so we tramped off in the pouring rain, through pools of water, no one knowing where to go or what was going to happen. Everyone was naturally most awfully depressed, but at last, about 5a.m., the regiment found itself together again, and when it got light we saw that all the force had collected round and about the same spot. Everyone was hungry and miserable, soaked to the skin and dog tired. As for myself and half my company this was our second night with no sleep. Directly it got light, everyone looked anxiously towards the camp and the position which the Boers had occupied beyond, but there was no sign of them anywhere. About 7 a.m., we got the cheering news that the force at Ladysmith had utterly defeated the Boers at Elandslaagte, and we presumed by this had relieved us, and then didn't we cheer! (Note 2)

At Elandslaagte on that day, the day after Talana, a force commanded by Major General John French severely mauled Jan Kock's force of Johannesburg Boers and foreign volunteers. They had advanced in contravention of Joubert's orders, well forward of any Boer forces on their flanks. Euphoric at the capture of a supply train on its way to Dundee, as previously related, they were attacked in their strong defensive position by infantry under the command of Brigadier General Ian Hamilton. Driven off the hill behind the station, the fugitives were attacked by the British cavalry who had been lying in wait for them. A squadron each of the 5th Lancers and the 5th Dragoon Guards charged the helpless and unsuspecting Boers who were in full retreat anyway, and totally routed them. Those who survived this frightful experience made it back to Dannhauser the next morning to alarm the Commandant General with their stories. (Note 3)

Early on the morning of Sunday 22nd October, Churcher and the rest of the men received the news of Elandslaagte:

> About 7 a.m. we got the cheering news that the force at Ladysmith had utterly defeated the Boers at Elandslaagte, and we presumed by this had relieved us, and then didn't we cheer! The first thing one of my men said to me was, "Ah, sir, can't we go and pay out the beggars who fired on us? So there was lots of spirit left in the men yet. (Note 4)

The senior officers had already met with Yule, now promoted Major General. Colonel F.R.C. Carleton of the Royal Irish Fusiliers, his brother, Colonel G.D. Carleton of the Leicestershire Regiment and some others were present. Also at the meeting was Colonel

John Dartnell of the Natal Mounted Police, an ex-British officer who had commanded this force for some years and, crucially, knew the area intimately. Clearly Dundee was indefensible and an immediate withdrawal to Ladysmith was unquestionably the only alternative. Ammunition was short, particularly artillery rounds, and about enough only for one more fight. Orders were made out for the retreat but not issued – the smashing success of the force sent out from Ladysmith against General Jan Kock's commando at Elandslaagte seemed to have radically changed the situation, as Churcher and almost the entire force were to assume. (Note 5)

Although the Boers had cut the direct telegraph line between Dundee and Ladysmith, they neglected to cut the line between Dundee and Helpmekaar and further, to Greytown and Pietermaritzburg. This was the route that messages were sent which seems not to have occasioned much, if any delay. The Postmaster of Dundee was Mr H.H. Paris, a Liverpudlian of some 33 years of age. He turned out to be one of the heroes of Talana as this account describes:

> Favouring winged collars and ties with knots four inches across, he was tall and a bit of a swell. Monocled, with carefully barbered curly hair, his generous moustache was neatly clipped. Educated at Liverpool College, he trained as a Telegraphist in the Liverpool Post Office where he caught the eye of the Postmaster. An opportunity arose for a Telegraphist in South Africa and Paris was offered a recommendation should he care to apply for the position in Durban Post Office. This he did successfully and spent a couple of years in Durban before being invited to take the position at Pietermaritzburg of Private Secretary to the Postmaster-General of Natal. His next step took Mr. Paris to Dundee and the position of Postmaster. General Penn-Symons commanded the British forces in the district and, hoping to invest the town, the Boers arrived in strength on 19 October. In this threatening situation Paris decided to sleep in his office and early the following morning he was rudely awakened by one of his clerks to be told that the Boers had commenced operations. They could be seen crowding the hills to the east of the town and, dressing hurriedly, the Postmaster was in time to see the first enemy shells over shooting the Post Office as the Boers tried to find the range of the army camp.
>
> Orders were given to leave the town and Paris tells of the march through torrential rain in pitch darkness. General Yule was now commanding and hoped for reinforcements. He asked Paris to return to the town and send various messages by telegraph. As the Postmaster rode into Dundee with two or three of his staff they came under fire from two 40-pounder guns. The Boers hesitated to enter the town and were content to fire at any sign of activity. "The shells went whizzing over the office and you may be certain I got the messages sent as soon as possible."
>
> Paris made three more trips back into town, telegraphing Ladysmith and Pietermaritzburg, each time attracting the attention of the Boer observers. The following morning, 22 October, Yule asked him to make a final journal to his post office to destroy all military messages. Unable to obtain horses, the small party of postal workers had to go on foot, but Yule assured them that he would send a mounted Orderly to inform them should the troops march out. "We kept up telegraphic communication with Pietermaritzburg. The Postmaster-General congratulated us on sticking to our posts to the last. The Camp Field Telegraph had bolted the day before." (Note 6)

Yule concluded that he now lay in the direct path of flight of the Boer fugitives from Elandslaagte. In fact they had fled much further to the west and only one wounded Boer, who had been pushed in a trolley along the line to Glencoe station, was captured. (Note 7)

Orders were now issued for a substantial force to head for the Glencoe Pass, the main road to Ladysmith and the pass over the Biggarsberg through which the rail line was routed. The expectation was the possibility of linking up with the further advance of the victorious British from Elandslaagte. However, the Heidelberg and Boksburg commandos under Commandant J.D. Weilbach, had now finally moved forward from Dannhauser and were strongly placed on the spur of Impati which runs south east to the pass. The 18th Hussars as the advance guard came under fire from the Boer guns from Impati. This made it impossible to seize the pass as, in addition, the Boers now held the ridge directly commanding the exit, the very ridge that the Hussars had occupied when they first arrived at Dundee. The British artillery, outranged by at least two thousand yards, was unable to silence the fire from Impati, and any movement of the baggage in the direction of Glencoe would have been within range of the Boer guns.

The force was back in the camp under Indumeni at 1 p.m. Yule had reluctantly to decide to retire on Ladysmith while there was still an open road. That evening a message arrived from White, confirming what had been stated in the telegram of the previous day from his staff, "I cannot reinforce you without sacrificing Ladysmith and the Colony behind. You must try and fall back on Ladysmith. I will do what I may to help you when you are nearer." This message may have been delivered to Yule by dispatch riders from Helpmekaar. It is not clear just when the telegraph machine in the Dundee post office was rendered inoperative by the postmaster that morning. (Note 8)

Not quite all the force sent out to Glencoe made it back to the new camp site. Major H.T. Laming of the 18th Hussars, commander of 'C' Squadron, led the advance as the force headed towards the Glencoe Pass. At the head was No. 4 Troop under the command of Acting Sergeant Major James Baldry. The Troop turned down the pass but, the main British force turned back after coming under fire, and Baldry and his men were unable to return up the pass to rejoin their comrades. There were Boer riflemen on both sides of the road now, the men of the Germiston commando having crossed over to the east and seen their first action, as J.F. Naudé describes: (translated from the Afrikaans)

> On Sunday morning the enemy made a move in the direction of Glencoe and obliged us to defend our positions. Our guns kept the enemy's at a respectful distance, so that all his shots were far too short and sank into the soft ground. The Heidelbergers now occupied the hills further to the south and when Commandant Weilbach required a patrol of burgers to occupy the summit of a hill to the south of Dundee, we offered ourselves. And thus twenty Germistoners went through a stream which flowed in a deep cleft between two mountains, to climb the steep mountain, with the railway at its foot, on the other side.
>
> When we got to the first wide edge of the hill, we saw a patrol of about 25 approaching from the south. We took up a position and waited for them. When they were about 500 or 600 yards to the left, they caught sight of us, took to their heels and sped into the hills. Then there was such a rumbling and crackle of Mausers.
>
> I will not easily forget that Sunday midday. When I lay there and the burgers were already firing on the fleeing English, for a few moments I underwent a violent struggle. The idea that I should shoot at a fellow man with the object of killing him – a fellow man who I had never seen before, against whom I had no bad feeling and who had personally done me no harm, aroused in me a feeling of remorse. And even though I was convinced of the justice of our cause and encouraged the burgers to fight, prayed for blessing on our weapons and was prepared to go together with our burgers, wherever duty would call. But now to take aim at a fellow man – even though an Englishman – just as I had often done to a buck, was more difficult for me than I had thought. (Note 9)

Baldry and his troop could not do other than head down the pass towards Ladysmith. The report of his commanding officer, Major Laming states that Baldry's troop reached Waschbank, "only to find that the lower ground was already in possession of considerable numbers of the enemy." There were in fact only a few Boers in Waschbank. Baldry headed back up the pass, encountered more Boers, but headed westwards, managed to cross the hills and bivouac for the night near where the Sundays River crosses the Dundee-Ladysmith road. He was at Elandslaagte station on Monday morning and was told that there were parties of the enemy between him and Ladysmith. These were some of the Free State Boers who had occupied the hills overlooking the farm Rietfontein that night. A patrol including a man who would later become one of the most remarkable of the Boer guerilla leaders, Christiaan de Wet, was certainly in the vicinity that morning. (Note 10)

The troop encountered the Boers at a level crossing and one of Baldry's men's horses was shot. A train, coming up the line bearing a white flag, was on a mission to recover the body of Colonel John Scott Chisholm, killed at Elandslaagte two days previously. Baldry stopped the train and warned them that the line had been torn up a little way further. Some of the men had a train ride back into Ladysmith but Baldry marched his men to safety without any further opposition. "In view of the signal service rendered by Sergeant Baldry, the Commander-in-Chief conferred the award of the Distinguished Conduct Medal on this non-commissioned officer." Corporal Padwick, with Private Clegg, on patrol ahead of the troop were unable to find their way back to the troop. They had a number of encounters with Boers. Padwick was captured and sent to Pretoria, while Private Clegg, wounded in one of the clashes, was sent into Dundee to join the other British wounded. Later on 2nd November five of the more seriously wounded were sent by train and ambulance to Ladysmith, the Boers not able to treat them in the field. Private Clegg did manage to survive the experience. (Note 11)

General Yule clearly intended that the casualties would be buried on Sunday evening, 22nd October at the foot of the Talana hill. The Reverend Gerard Bailey received a request to be at the foot of the hill at 6 p.m. but Boer fire and the incessant rain prevented that from happening. On Monday evening, General Penn Symons died and was buried in St James's Churchyard the next day. The burials at Smith's farm at the foot of Talana took place only on Wednesday, once the Boers had occupied the town. (Note 12)

The civilian population of Dundee had almost all left the town. They made their way to various farms in the vicinity or started along the roads to Ladysmith or Helpmekaar. The *Natal Mercury* correspondent reported the situation to his newspaper:

> When the troops had moved out of range the Boers devoted their attention to the town, and sent several shells into it. Two went over the station and did some damage to a dwelling house, while others were directed to the magazine, showing the knowledge the Boers had of the buildings in the town. At the time the shells were fired the mist was gradually setting on the hills, and by 5 o'clock heavy rain fell and shelling ceased. There was naturally much apprehension in town, and although there was no hysterical panic, people fled to every available place of apparent shelter, in case the Boers renewed the attack.
>
> Shortly after, an officer came into town with a message from the General to the Chairman of the Local Board, stating that everyone was to leave the town within 10 minutes. Mr Ryley, chairman of the Board, accompanied by Mr Escombe, rode out to the General to get instructions from him as to the safest place to send the people. As they came driving back they were met by the outgoing crowd of people who had no idea where they were going. Messers, Ryley and Escombe shouted as they drove in: "Go to Decker's Farm, and wait there until you get a further message." This was imperfectly heard by the majority, who went trudging on, and got to different places.
>
> It was raining hard and pitch dark. The roads were ankle deep in mud and water. Several women and children who had not left the town before were among the fugitives – and they rushed along with the rest – getting into barbed wire fences, sluits, and mud holes. We wandered right into the middle of a patrol, who conducted us to Rowan's Farm, which we found already crowded with members of the Town Guard and a Carbineer patrol. Mr Rowan left his farm a few days before and the crowd was in full possession. There was nothing to eat, and nothing to drink but water. Every room was filled with men lying on the floor, sitting on the tables, and under them. The stable was crowded, and others were on the verandah.
>
> Every newcomer was asked if he had any message from town as to what they were to do, but nobody knew except that some… (Note 13)

Since taking over command, Yule had done his best under the invidious circumstances that were not of his making. He was dead against retreating, abandoning the wounded, including the mortally wounded General Penn Symons, the stores and the inhabitants of the town. There were few alternatives to be considered after White had ordered him to retreat into Ladysmith. White desperately needed the men of the Glencoe Field Force, Penn Symons's ill-conceived venture, to reinforce the garrison in Ladysmith. Even more vital were the eighteen guns of the three RFA batteries. Yule now issued the orders that had been drafted that morning and at 4 p.m. the regimental commanders were counseled that the march to Ladysmith must be undertaken that night under the strictest secrecy. Once it was dark, Major Wickham, one of the officers of the Commissariat, took thirty-three wagons back to the old camp. Somehow they were not seen by the Boers and busied themselves with loading up as much stores and materiel as they could in the limited time available. Their orders were to move off through the town and await the force on the Helpmekaar road at the Dundee Collieries. Two companies of the Leicestershire Regiment provided the escort to counter any unwelcome interference from the Boers. (Note 14)

The direct route down the Glencoe Pass was blocked by the Boers but, strangely, the Boers had taken no steps to close off the road to the south leading to Helpmekaar and Greytown. Neither the road nor the telegraph connection had been cut. Colonel John Dartnell was their guide and at 9 p.m. on Sunday evening the march began. (Note 16)

Notes on sources:
1. Burnett *The 18th Hussars in South Africa* p26.
2. Churcher *With the Irish Fusiliers from Alexandria to Natal 1899-1900* p21.
3. Maurice *History of the war in South Africa* Vol 1 pp157-471 has one of the numerous accounts of the Battle of Elandslaagte. It was in this battle that John French first came to prominence. The charge on the Boer fugitives by the cavalry was an inglorious gallop against fleeing and near-helpless Boers scattering across the flat plain to the north of Elandslaagte. Anglesey *A History of the British Cavalry Volume IV 1899-1913* gives a detailed account and the author's conclusions. Ian Hamilton was Brigadier General as commander of an infantry brigade.
4. Churcher *With the Irish Fusiliers from Alexandria to Natal 1899-1900* p21.
5. Yule had received a telegram at 4 p.m. on 21st October, "with the compliments of Sir George

The camp of the Royal Irish Fusiliers on 21st October at dawn – supposedly out of range of the Boer guns on Impati, in the left background. Talana is on the right.

"Map No I : The country around Ladysmith and Dundee"
(from Burnett, *The 18th Hussars in South Africa*)
The route of the 18th Hussars on their advance to Dundee is shown as well as that of their withdrawal back to Ladysmith.

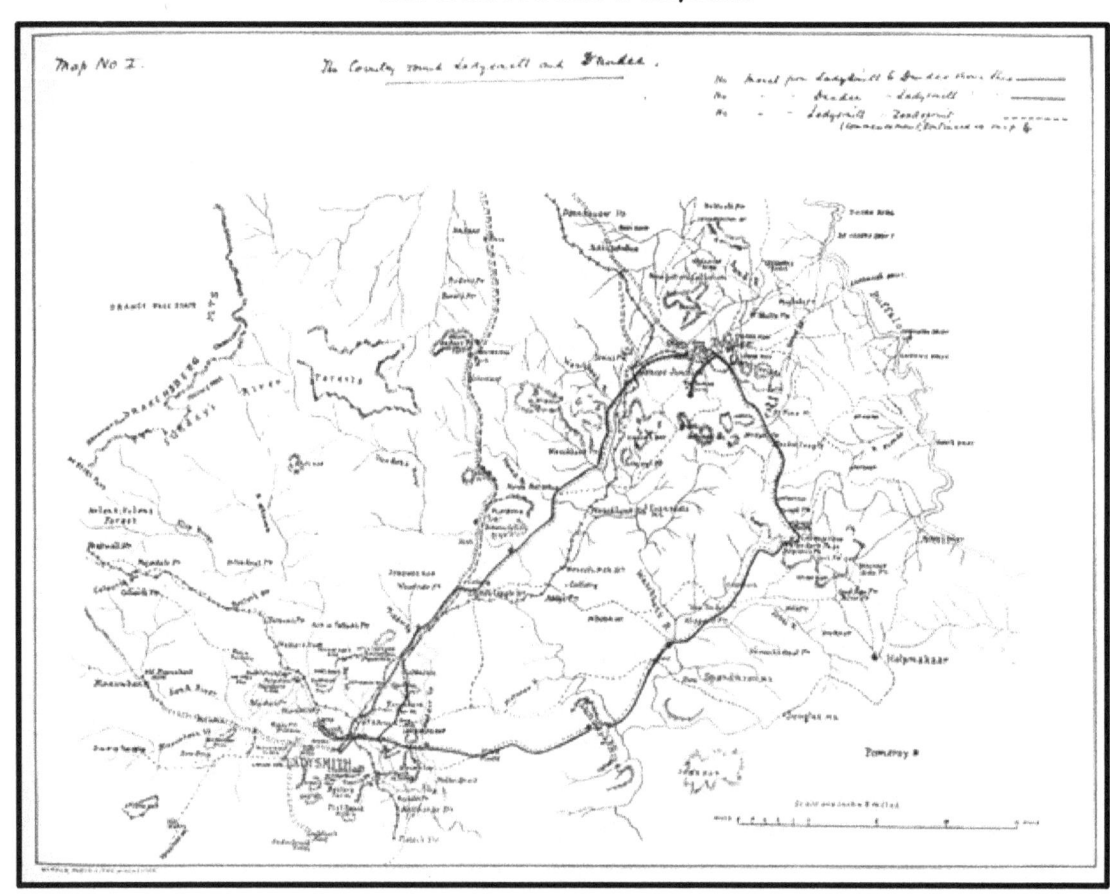

White" congratulating him "upon his appointment to the rank of Major General." Maurice, *History of the war in South Africa* Vol 1 p143. Certainly, just then, Yule would have preferred reinforcements to promotion!

6. From a contemporary article entitled "The Simple Man" quoted in the Spink catalogue of a sale of Anglo Boer War medals and ephemera in 1999. The article was offered together with a Queen's South Africa 1899-1902 medal with no clasp. The article originally appeared in *Pen Pictures of the War* by Men at the Front, published in 1900. Maurice *History of the war in South Africa* Vol 1 p144 says that: "At 8 a.m., October 22nd, two dispatch riders arriving from Helpmekaar delivered a message from the Prime Minister of Natal, announcing a victory on the previous day at Elandslaagte." This particular message may well have been sent after the Postmaster had severed the link.

7. Maurice *History of the war in South Africa* Vol 1 p145. Naudé *Veg en Vlug* p38 tells of capturing a man hiding in a ditch after the Hussars had been driven away. He was unarmed, did not wear khaki and could not speak English (and presumably Afrikaans as well). Naudé thought he might be a German fugitive from Elandslaagte and sent him to the commandant in case he had "some mischief up his sleeve."

8. Maurice *History of the war in South Africa* Vol 1 p146.

9. Naudé *Veg en Vlug* p38.

10. Christiaan de Wet *Three Years' War* p17.

11. Burnett *The 18th Hussars in South Africa* pp29-31. The journey of the more seriously wounded to Ladysmith, including a stop at Pepworth's farm, Rietfontein, converted into a hospital by the Boers, is described by one of the them on pp39-40.

12. Bailey *Seven months under Boer rule* p64.

13. *The Natal Mercury*, Friday, October 27, 1899. "Mr Escombe" was of course Harry Escombe, an ex-Prime Minister of Natal – he had (or had acquired) a spider and horses and managed somehow to make his way back to Ladysmith.

14. Amery *The Times History of the war in South Africa* Vol II pp199-200. Maurice *History of the war in South Africa* Vol 1 p146. The Dundee Collieries, on the outskirts of town, still operate in 2009.

15. John Dartnell was a retired army officer in 1874 when he first arrived in Natal. He helped in the formation of the Natal Mounted Police and became its first commander. The NMP was a para-military force and the first line of defence for the Colony. By the time of the outbreak of the Anglo Boer war in 1899, it had become the Natal Police and John Dartnell, now promoted Colonel, was its commander.

Chapter 5

The march begins
22 to 24 October 1899

"I could hear the tramping of horses, as if a large body were passing."
(From the Reverend Gerard Bailey's journal entry for 22 October)

On Friday the Glencoe Field Force had won a victory over the Boers, pushing them off a strong position on Talana Hill. All the training done by the British army at Aldershot had come into play – first the artillery bombardment, a frontal assault by the infantry and then mopping up by the cavalry – they had won a resounding victory, but at unacceptable cost. Symons was the architect of both the victory and the tactics that were the cause of the force losing more than ten per cent of its strength in the frontal assault up the steep, rocky slope – and in a botched cavalry operation. On Sunday, only two days later, Yule's little army certainly were not enjoying any fruits of their victory. They were clustered together on a stony hillside, barely out of range of the Boers' big guns on the mountain of Impati. Short of food, since most of the commissariat was under fire in the vacated camp, not even enough ammunition for one more engagement and no properly secure water supply.

Major Churcher tells of how things were on Sunday afternoon:

> By this time it was common to the most non-military mind that affairs were in a bad state. We have not enough ammunition for more than one engagement, and they say that Sir George White has sent a message that he cannot help us. They held a council of war in the evening and happily fixed on the only way out of the difficulty. We march this evening with such transport as we have, loaded with rations, make a detour to the S.E. and try and get around Glencoe to Ladysmith. Colonel Dartnell has offered to lead us, and if there is any man who could do it he could, as he is head of the Natal Police, and has been in Natal pretty near all his life, I believe. We have to abandon the camp, all our kits and mess stores, in fact, everything must be sacrificed to food and ammunition. No one has got even a change of socks. The whole thing is most ghastly, especially as we are obliged to leave all our sick and wounded behind, including General Penn Symons. (Note 1)

The wonder is that Churcher could find the time to write in such detail about their situation as he sat among the stones under a waterproof sheet in the downpour. Some of the men had not even this piece of kit to keep off the rain. Another man, a Gunner in the 13th Battery Royal Field Artillery, William Netley, also kept a diary in his haversack and he wrote about the rules imposed on the marchers:

> In the dead of night we are on the move. Strict orders against striking matches, and no talking aloud. I would not have minded the talking part of the business being stopped but to have to go without a smoke puts my pipe properly out. Of course it was the correct thing to do as a light would have shown the Bores (sic) what we are up to. (Note 2)

The route from their makeshift camp took them through the eastern part of town. The inhabitants had almost all left, dispersed mostly to nearby farms. Some had gone on horseback to Greytown or the railway south of Ladysmith according to Reverend Gerard Bailey. About the only people left were Bailey himself and Father Murray, the Catholic priest attached to the Dublins as Chaplain, as well as the Postmaster asleep next to his telegraph machine. The two churchmen had had a busy day with the sad work of funerals and "had struck up a companionship." The Catholic Church was located in a somewhat safer part of town than St James's Anglican Church and Gerard Bailey's vicarage. "The sisters of the convent had left plenty of blankets and pillows, so we were able to make ourselves very comfortable." They slept in a space behind the altar and Bailey woke about 11 p.m.:

> Some noise outside had roused me. I listened. I could hear the tramping of horses, as if a large body were passing. I walked to the window and looked out. It was a dark night but ten yards away I could see our infantry – the cavalry had now passed by – marching along quietly and at a steady pace. After the infantry came the transport. What a time the wagons took! What delays and stopping there were! In my sleepy state I half imagined the enemy were pursuing. I fumed and fretted and grew terribly impatient. How obstinate the oxen and mules appeared to be. How stupid the drivers and voorloopers. The whole busy scene became a regular nightmare to me. The Roman Catholic church is situated at a corner where two roads meet. Wagons were coming down both roads and meeting here, hence so many stoppages.

> An officer stood at the corner. He was most indefatigable in his efforts to hurry the transport along. "Now then, what are you stopping for?" – "Where's the driver of that wagon?" – "Will you get along there?" – I don't remember the last of the wagons – I fell asleep. (Note 3)

The Postmaster had been assured by Yule that "he would send a mounted Orderly to inform them should the troops march out." In fact they had been forgotten and it was only by chance that they were not left behind:

> Shortly before midnight a military scout saw lights at the Post Office and rode up to investigate. Surprised to find civilians still in Dundee, he told Paris that the troops had pulled out. Yule had forgotten all about his devoted civilian telegraphists. "We soon had the lights out after cramming the registered letters in the safe and carrying away what cash and stamps we could, amounting to £200."
> They caught up the last wagon and walked in the rain, splashing through mud and slush. (Note 4)

The old British camp, once it became visible through the mist on Monday morning 23rd October, was "so swarming with wounded and hospital personnel that Colonel Trichardt was under the impression that Yule and all his troops had returned." Trichardt seems to have used this to justify opening fire on the British hospital and its Red Cross flag, claiming later that the flag was invisible. Whether only one shell landed among the wounded in the hospital tents, as the Boers later claimed, or whether it was a regular fusillade, as the British claimed, cannot now be determined. However, Major Donegan, in command of the 18th Field Hospital and the senior British officer present, sent one of his captains up the stoney path up Impati to surrender the hospital in the interest of their patients. It was now around 10.30 a.m. and Donegan, reluctant to give away the news of Yule's secret departure, had been forced to act in the interests of his patients. (Note 5)

The Boers were at first still hesitant to enter the town and it was afternoon before the Reverend Bailey watched their entry into Dundee:

> About 1 o'clock they came pouring in. Every man was mounted, on small hardy horses, although here and there one thought one recognized the fine steeds they had captured from the Hussars. The enemy were of every age, from the stripling of sixteen to the white-bearded patriarch. The horses were in excellent condition, and these fellows can ride. They are the Texan cowboys of South Africa. It is very seldom you see them walking or trotting, it is always the triple or the canter.
> They wore no uniform, except here and there one of the Staats Artillerie, but rough serviceable clothes, with top boots or leggings, and soft felt hats. Their rifles they carried slung over their backs and all had bandoliers filled with cartridges. I saw one Boer who had on a belt as well as two bandoliers, carrying 243 cart-ridges in all. When they entered the town they seemed to be in some trepidation as if they expected a trap laid for them, for they quickly cantered into every part of the town to satisfy themselves. As to the whereabouts of the troops they were completely nonplussed. (Note 6)

Yule's column had marched through the night and at dawn they were nearly twelve miles away from the Boers in Dundee, as Major Burnett of the 18th Hussars tells:

> No opposition to our march was encountered, and at daybreak part of the 18th Hussars and two batteries crossed Blesboklaagte and took up a position on the far side to cover the crossing of the whole force. The ravine was passed and the column halted for breakfast, at about 9 a.m. for two hours, about a mile on the far side of the spruit, the infantry tired out with their long night march after the work they had to do on the preceding day. (Note 7)

Yule had seen to it that the telegraph line to Greytown was cut outside Dundee. Now, just past Blesboklaagte, either the military telegraphist or the Dundee Postmaster, Mr Paris, was able to hook up to the line on the farm Dewaas. They reported their progress to General White, anxiously awaiting some definite information in Ladysmith. In Dundee, a part of the garrison had been a troop of Natal Carbineers under Captain Charlie Willson. He had asked for, and been given, permission to take some of his men back to Ladysmith independent of the column. They made it back without encountering any Boer patrols on their journey. They were the first soldiers from Dundee into Ladysmith with first-hand news of Yule's successful evasion of the Transvaalers. (Note 8)

Certainly, Trichardt on Impati could see the British column in the far distance, as will be related in the next chapter. They may have tried signaling by heliograph in the belief that what they had sighted was Meyer's commando. Burnett apparently saw signals during the daytime halt past Blesboklaagte:

> Only a two hour halt was allowed here, as we were still in sight of Impati Mountain, from which the Boers were signaling to us, mistaking

us for some of their own people coming up from the Vryheid district. (Note 9)

However, according to Major C.F. Romer of the Royal Dublin Fusiliers, the Boers were signaling to a local farmer that night by heliograph – but the story must surely be apocryphal:

> During the night a mysterious heliograph was seen twinkling and blinking away on the left flank. After some difficulty it was ascertained that it was communicating with the farm of a man named Potgieter, professedly a British subject. He was, in fact, caught in flagrante delicto in full communication with the unknown Boer signaller, and paid for his crime with his life. (Note 10)

The column moved on after the halt for breakfast and passed Beith and the little Dutch church next to the road on the farm Vlakfontein. They stopped again at the head of the Van Tonder's Nek pass while the 18th Hussars and some of the Colonials scouted the two possible roads down the escarpment of the Biggarsberg. Major Churcher took two photographs of the bivouac which have survived and seem to show the column at rest on the slope just north of the church. There are two roads down the steep mountainside and the decision was taken to use Van Tonder's Nek pass, which is further to the south and thus more distant from the Boers. Yule's telegram of that morning indicated that the Beith road was going to be used but its steepness and sharp turns would have been difficult for the transport to negotiate, even though it would have shortened the distance back to Ladysmith. Once the roads had been scouted, the march continued, the first elements entering the top of the pass at 11 p.m. (Note 11)

There was continual worry and concern that the Boers were planning to attack the column. Churcher articulates this in his diary for Tuesday 24th October:

> We got down the pass through the Biggarsberg luckily without encountering any of the enemy, as it was a most awkward place to be caught in, and a few determined men on the hills round could have played old Harry. We marched till about 10 a.m. but, being rear guard, our progress was very slow, and by the time we had got to (the) Waschbank (River), where the remainder of the force were halted, the two leading regiments had been in hours and were all bathing in a stream. We are all of us getting very thin and hungry looking, as all there is to eat is bully beef and biscuits with muddy water to drink, and no sleep since the 20th. We were taking our turn at bathing and cleaning up, when the alarm went round that the Boers were coming, so we took up a position to meet them. No Boers appeared, luckily for us I suppose, although we held an excellent position. The whole morning we have been hearing heavy gun firing in the direction of Ladysmith, but it ceased about 2.30 p.m., and we are wondering how things have gone with Sir George White. (Note 12)

The infantry remained in place all day in a ridge on the left bank of the river, but not the Irish Fusiliers, who had moved back to the other side of the river once the alarm was over. In the late afternoon there was a huge thunderstorm, the river rose six feet in an hour, trapping the Royal Dublin Fusiliers and a few of the 18th Hussars on the wrong side. Major Romer of the Dublins explained what happened:

> ...the river was again forded at 4 p.m., and only just in time. A violent thunderstorm burst, and the water rose ten feet in two hours. 'H' company, under Lieutenant Shewan, and a patrol of the 18th Hussars were left on the north bank, and were thus cut off from the main body for several hours. It rained in torrents until 11 p.m., and the battalion, formed in quarter-column, had to lie down in pools of water, and get what sleep it could. (Note 13)

Yule himself led two batteries of artillery, the 67th and 69th RFA, two squadrons of 18th Hussars and some MI in the direction of the sound of the guns. After riding nine miles and still not seeing the Ladysmith troops, the battle being further away than they had thought, Yule gave the order to return to the Waschbank River. In any case, by 2 p.m. the distant firing had died away. They arrived back at sundown but without Lieutenant Clarke of the Hussars. Clarke had led a patrol of five men, including a colonial guide but had become separated from the main body. He describes what happened:

> Our object was to push on to some high ground about three miles beyond the main body, to try and discover a position for the guns to shell any Boers who might be retiring in front of Sir G. White. We discovered no signs of retreating Boers, though we pushed on some way beyond the high ground. We passed through Wessels Nek, which was deserted and looted, and commenced to withdraw about 3 p.m. Soon after this a terrific storm burst, the rain being so heavy it was impossible to see more than a few yards. Owing to this we lost our way, the guide knowing nothing of the country, and accounting for his ignorance by saying he had only lived ten years in the neighbourhood. Eventually, at 10 p.m., we again found ourselves

at Wessels Nek. We judged it safer to sleep on the veldt, which we did, keeping watch in turn. At daybreak we made another effort to find the column, but not being successful, I judged it best to strike for Ladysmith. We passed the battlefield of Elandslaagte, strewn with dead horses, and reached Elandslaagte Station about nine. Here we found a coolie (sic) cook, and although the place had been looted and used as a hospital, he managed to find us some cocoa and tinned fish. Pushing on, we reached a spot where the Modder runs under the railway. We saw a low kopje about 400 yards in front, which was covered with men. Looking at them through the glasses I saw they wore slouch hats, on which the guide at once said, "Oh! They are carbineers out to meet the column." At this moment two mounted men left the kopje and galloped out towards us. As they approached I saw they were Boers. I now saw we had fallen into a hornets' nest, and several more men were beginning to gallop up from the kopje. I took the only chance and we dashed down into the spruit, crossed the line under the bridge, and galloped for all we were worth. Fortunately no one seemed to think of pursuing us, as our horses were so beat that we had to dismount after about a mile. We saw no more Boers after this, and eventually reached the line of outposts thrown out by the 18th Hussars some six miles out of Ladysmith. (Note 14)

The weather was now the principal adversary and the rain was incessant throughout the night and Churcher commented that practically everyone was wet to the skin. He at least kept his head dry with an empty biscuit box into which he put his head and he got the regiment's chaplain to take another picture. Colonel John Dartnell now left, leaving some of his police to guide the column and galloped into Ladysmith. He arrived some time in the early afternoon to give White the news that Yule and his men were on their way and thus far, safe and had not seen any Boer pursuers.

White received intelligence about the column's escape from a number of other sources. Sergeant Baldry arrived in Ladysmith on 23rd October but he would have been able to shed very little light on what had happened to the column. (See Chapter 4) Lieutenant Clarke came in on the 25th and would have told of Yule's sortie. Another source was a prospector who had clearly decided that the war zone was no place to be looking for minerals:

> Mr F.C. Snaith, a cyclist who set out for Johannesburg with a cycle laden front and back with a prospector's tent, fly, hammock, two pairs of blankets, several changes of clothing, a change of boots, tinned meats, biscuits and bread, fruit, salt, and a map of South Africa, passed Yule's column on the march, and brought news of the retreat to General White.
>
> Arriving at Ladysmith, he was advised to go to see General White, to inform him with regard to the retreating army. He therefore went to the headquarters. On an Indian attendant indicating General White's room, the cyclist knocked at the door and a voice said "Come in." He entered and saw the General writing at a dressing-table. The apparition of the stranger had a disconcerting effect. The General cried, "Who are you? What do you want? What are you doing here?" and before the poor man could reply two aides-de-camp rushed in and planted his back against the door. Then both asked questions rapidly. The guilty man answered meekly that he had very properly knocked at the door and been told to come in, that he had come in, and he only wanted to give them some information. Then Sir George and the other officers cooled down, and, after hearing the information, cordially thanked him for his news. (Note 15)

Notes on sources:
1. Churcher *With the Irish Fusiliers from Alexandria to Natal 1899-1900* p22.
2. Gunner William Netley of the 13th Battery RFA kept a diary which Thomas Pakenham made use of in writing *The Boer War* and, additionally, interviewed him as a very old man in about 1968. My extract has the spelling corrected where necessary!
3. Bailey *Seven months under Boer rule* pp61-62.
4. From a contemporary article entitled "The Simple Man" – see Note 6 from Chapter 4.
5. Breytenbach, *Die Geskiedenis van die Tweede Vryheidsoorlog* Vol I p278.
6. Bailey *Seven months under Boer rule* pp63-64.
7. Burnett *The 18th Hussars in South Africa* pp40-41.
8. Bailey *Seven months under Boer rule* p64 mentions the Boers wanting to know the whereabouts of Charlie Willson when they entered the town on 23rd October – by then he and his troop were almost in Ladysmith.
9. Burnett, *The 18th Hussars in South Africa* p41.
10. Romer and Mainwaring *The Second Battalion Royal Dublin Fusiliers in the South African War* p19. This incident is something of a mystery and is not corroborated anywhere else. The summary execution of a Boer farmer, should it have happened, would certainly have been the subject of a vigorous protest from the Boer authorities.

11. Burnett *The 18th Hussars in South Africa* p41 apparently quotes the text of Yule's message to White sent from the farm Dewaas, just to the south of Blesboklaagte, where the force stopped for breakfast: "Propose camping at Beith today, and march to Sundays River, Beith-Ladysmith road, tomorrow, starting at 2 a.m."
12. Churcher *With the Irish Fusiliers from Alexandria to Natal* pp24-25. The gun firing that they heard was from Rietfontein, White's attempt to divert the attention of the Free Staters from Yule's column.
13. Romer and Mainwaring *The Second Battalion Royal Dublin Fusiliers in the South African War* p20.
14. Burnett *The 18th Hussars in South Africa* pp42-43.
15. *Pen Pictures of the War* pp82-83.

Chapter 6

The Boer advance on Ladysmith
24 to 26 October 1899

"Whatever the achievements of Yule and his men –
the chief credit for their escape must go to Joubert…"
(Pakenham, *The Boer War* p148)

The British frontal attack on the Boers on Talana and their subsequent withdrawal from Dundee evoked some surprising reactions from the Boer generals. The Commandant General, Piet Joubert, was alarmed from the very first at Kock's unauthorized foray to Elandslaagte station. Concerned that, should Kock have taken up a position at Waschbank Station, his small force, right in the path of Yule's men retreating to Ladysmith, would be surprised, attacked and annihilated. Consequently, at 5 a.m. on Sunday 21st October, he gave orders to Commandant Pretorius at Hattingspruit to send ten of his best riders to Waschbank to find Kock, warn him of Yule's approach and allow him to prepare for the clash. It was these men that Sergeant Baldry had seen (and avoided) at Waschbank. (Note 1)

Joubert knew nothing of the disaster that had befallen Kock at Elandslaagte until later in the morning of Sunday 22nd October. Receipt of this news alarmed Joubert even more. On Sunday morning there appeared at the Hattingspruit headquarters a steady stream of fugitives, and including Commandant Ben Viljoen, with harrowing stories of their utter defeat. General Kock was severely wounded and taken to Ladysmith by the British, the two guns which had been captured by the Boers from Jameson's raiders had been lost, and Kock's commandos were scattered and destroyed as a fighting force. President Kruger in Pretoria, considered (by the Boers) to be a military man of note, was equally disconcerted and ordered Joubert to concentrate his commandos around and on the summit of Impati, including those of Lucas Meyer and Schalk Burger, still on his way from Swaziland. This to be done so that the British would be unable to attack another part of the Transvaal force and defeat that too. Joubert was to ensure that the burgers did not suffer any shortage of ammunition or food. Kruger further trusted that God would lead the Commandant General and shield the burgers from harm. Kruger also called on President Steyn to order his Free State burgers forward and reprimanded him for the total lack of support that his men had provided to Kock at Elandslaagte. (Note 2)

Joubert, as a result of this setback and the messages from the President, was now having some doubts about the whole venture of the invasion of Natal. Up until then he had correctly interpreted Yule's moves as an attempt to rescue his threatened and battered Glencoe Field Force. He now thought that the British moves were an attempt to draw the Boers away from their mountain positions and overwhelm them when they occupied the town of Dundee. He no longer believed that Yule was fleeing Dundee but that he was attempting to confuse the Boers, and then surprise and overwhelm them when once they occupied the town. Meyer and Burger were told to join Erasmus on Impati mountain so as to ward off any attack. Erasmus, Trichardt and Weilbach were instructed to remain extremely watchful and he even sent them a message which said: (translated from the Dutch)

> The force from Lady Smith (sic) and the camp that you have seen on the other side of Dundee, could now advance right across the flat ground from Glencoe to Hatting Station and attack you from that side while the fleeing troops from Dundee could return and would thereby place you between two fires. (Note 3)

That Yule's four thousand man army with its guns and transport had managed to take the road to Helpmekaar without attracting the attention of the Boers on Impati, and the fire of their big guns, was astounding. The column was four miles long and must have taken two hours or more to pass through the eastern side of Dundee, making a sharp right turn at the Catholic Church, watched by the Reverend Bailey. The only explanation is that in the Boer camps on Impati there was disagreement and wrangling between the various officers. Admittedly, the weather was misty and rainy, but Commandant Weilbach and General Erasmus were at loggerheads. According to Joubert, Weilbach would no longer cooperate with Erasmus and Joubert went so far as to ask the Transvaal government to recall Weilbach and replace him with Commandant Schutte of the police, who had been left in Johannesburg to maintain law and order. Colonel Trichardt also expressed his opinion that Yule was allowed to escape because of a "lack of cooperation by the officers" and also requested that the "obstinate" Weilbach be removed. (Note 4)

The Commandant General, Piet Joubert at no time visited the camps of the various commandos on Impati or at Glencoe. Erasmus requested him on 22nd October to "come here immediately as quickly as possible. We require your advice and support concerning the right position to take up for an attack." From

Joubert's reply, that he was unable to proceed further than Hattingspruit, and that Erasmus, and if possible, Trichardt, should visit him there, it is clear he made no effort to visit the commandos. He did not personally inspect the camps so as to ascertain for himself the conditions there. Further, it was his responsibility to make sure that his officers had closed off all escape routes to the south – this he did not do. Only through the Commandant General's personal presence and his "great experience, skill and influence" would "the general dissatisfaction and demoralization disappear, the pressing dangers be turned away and the war operations put on the right footing." This was the opinion of Jan Smuts "and almost all intelligent people." (Note 5)

During the morning of 23rd October, even before the occupation of Dundee, Trichardt on Impati noticed troops on the heights of the Biggarsberg. He was unable to decide whether they were heading for Greytown or awaiting reinforcements from Ladysmith. He reported this to the Commandant General. He also sent fifty of his artillerymen to Biggarsbergnek to watch their movements. Erasmus added fifty of his men and later sent a one hundred and fifty man patrol to the same place. Joubert was still very concerned about the possibility of an attack on Dundee, and a decisive battle, by forces from Ladysmith now combined with Yule's men. He was concerned that the forces of the Free State and Transvaal should combine in an attack on Yule's force. He sent messages to the Chief Commandant of the Orange Free State, Marthinus Prinsloo in this regard. Prinsloo said that he just needed to be told where the pass was which was holding up the British so that he could send a commando there. Yule's army would then be between two Boer forces and easily eliminated. (Note 6)

However, Joubert was now becoming convinced that the Elandslaagte reverse suffered by the Boers was not as serious as he had first thought. Various people had appeared who had been thought to have been killed and they convinced him that it was not the awful disaster that he had first thought it to be. He now sent a message to Trichardt on 23rd October that described his new feelings about Elandslaagte: (translated from the Dutch)

> It was just a small group of people who had a hard fight against an overwhelming force, that already was upon them until they realised that they had together almost 20 cannons firing on them when they had only 2. (Note 7)

Erasmus, Trichardt and Weilbach, in contrast, took little notice of their commander's fear and trepidation and made preparations to occupy Dundee. On 23rd October, the day that Joubert expected to be attacked, Erasmus's commandos were in the ridges around Dundee and Weilbach had moved his men towards Indumeni, the high mountain south of Dundee. They were thus to the west of and close to the site of the last British camp. Meyer still had not changed his position to the east of Talana as Erasmus had ordered him to remain there so as to assail the expected British attack on their right flank. Colonel Trichardt, with his artillery, remained on Impati. Once the weather improved and the mist cleared away, Trichardt opened fire with his guns, and Major Donegan requested the Boers to cease fire as the wounded in the hospital were the only British soldiers left, as previously related. Joubert's orders were that no one should enter Dundee except those sent in by order of General Erasmus to get food and ammunition. (Note 8)

This order only reached Erasmus after he had already sent a ten-man patrol into Dundee to ascertain that the British really had left. This is how Reitz described the patrol:

> As Maroola (Erasmus) was not quite certain that the English evacuation was complete, he sent a patrol of ten men forward to investigate. My brother and I were of the party, and, while we were riding ahead along the base of a kopje, we saw half a dozen English soldiers running up the slope about 500 yards off. We shouted to them to stop, but as they paid no heed, we sprang to the ground and fired, bringing two men down. The others now halted, and, riding up, we found one dead and another badly wounded. The rest told us they were a signaling party that had lost their way in the rains and mists of the preceding day, and they seemed greatly taken aback when they heard that their troops had evacuated Dundee.
>
> We left the dead man lying where he fell and ordered the prisoners to carry their wounded companion into town, and as we were anxious to be first in, we left them and rode on.
>
> By now Maroola's men were also making for Dundee, galloping hard behind us, but we were well in advance and easily got in before they came. They were not long, however, and soon 1,500 men were whooping through the streets, and behaving in a very undisciplined manner. Officers tried to stem the rush, but we were not to be denied, and we plundered shops and dwelling-houses, and did considerable damage before the Commandants and Field Cornets were able to restore some semblance of order. (Note 9)

On the other side of town, Weilbach's men were at first equally wary. J.F. Naudé tells of their cautious approach: (translated from the Afrikaans)

> We did not actually know if the whole enemy force had flown or whether a part had stayed behind, therefore we approached somewhat carefully. Near the town there were a few horses, and to find out if the enemy was still in the town, we had the opportunity to go and fetch them. They would be given to the burgers. Very quickly the horses which the English had left behind were in our hands. I christened mine "Dundee."
>
> The burgers now streamed into town. A few of us went through the town to the place where the English camp stood originally and where there were still a few tents. How surprised we were when we saw a number of English walking around among the tents! And they all looked at us. So then we wondered what we should do. But we walked to the camp where we met the wounded, with doctors and nurses. We got into conversation with a young officer and he was amazed to hear that we were Boers. He wanted to know what would happen to them, how they would be treated, and much more. What did he expect from a Boer!
>
> While the discussion was in progress, two burgers arrived by order of General Joubert to guard the camp. In one of the tents we found 30 Lee Metfords, just as many revolvers, ten sabres and two bandoliers. For the small service which I had luckily rendered here, I obtained a beautiful sabre and revolver. (Note 10)

Far from now being terrified of a British attack, Joubert now gave orders to all his officers in Dundee to advance southwards in the direction of Ladysmith. Nonetheless his orders included instructions that they should all act together so as to avoid another debacle such as occurred to Kock. Erasmus, Trichardt and Weilbach immediately set about obeying this order and the Long Tom was taken down from Impati (no easy task) and entrained at Glencoe. The forces now concentrated at Glencoe and Schalk Burger finally appeared with his three hundred men and three guns. Meyer complained that his animals were in no condition to chase after the British, now known to have fled down the road to Helpmekaar. It was only on 24th October that he set off after them.

Joubert now decided to split his force into two. The one part was to drive straight through to Ladysmith and link up with the Free Staters, while Meyer was to take command of the other part and chase after Yule. On the 25th October Joubert sent another one hundred men to reinforce Meyer and at the same time sent a five hundred man commando by another route to attempt to cut off the British. Meyer's animals, it is said, were in a much worse condition than Yule's and were unable to match his pace. By this time Yule was within the protection of the Ladysmith garrison. In view of the fact that Meyer and his men had been stationary not far east of Talana for three days or more, this seems surprising. There is also no information that the two parties of men sent by Joubert sighted the British or came anywhere close. (Note 11)

Dietlof van Warmelo, a member of the Pretoria commando, part of which was sent to reinforce Lucas Meyer, records his experience and wry comment:

> When our commando left Dundee to move in the direction of Ladysmith, part of the Pretoria town commando was sent to reinforce Lucas Meyer, who was to follow the troops fleeing from Dundee with his commando. My brother and I went with it. A terrible thunderstorm came on just then, and during the whole march to Ladysmith it rained heavily. Every moment we expected to come up with the troops, but they had too great a start, and we did not overtake them at all. We were too late again. An English General has said that "the Boers are brave, and make good plans, but are always twenty-four hours late". That can be explained in this way. We were accustomed to fighting against Kaffirs, (sic) who hid in the woods and mountains, and against whom we had to advance with the utmost precaution, so as to lose as few lives as possible. So we were too cautious in the beginning of the war. We would not make a great sacrifice to win a battle. (Note 12)

The Boer commanders, at this initial stage of the war, were older men, prominent politicians and citizens of the various towns. Many had had a great deal of military experience in campaigns against the native tribes in both republics. Almost every year since their formation, the Republics had been in conflict with their indigenous inhabitants. (Note 13) Piet Joubert, the Commandant General of the Transvaal, had a permanent appointment and a salary from the government, but other Generals and Commandants were elected by their fellow citizens. Undoubtedly, many of these, and Louis Botha is but one example, had outstanding military ability. Roland Schikkerling's comments on the leadership in the early part of the war are telling:

> It is useless to linger on the dilatory methods of General Joubert and of the other older officers. Through their excessive caution and inability to adapt themselves speedily enough to the new

conditions, and to take advantage of the splendid opportunities which the first days of the war in Natal offered, as well as through their contempt for the advice of younger and brisker men, they contributed to our failure. (Note 14)

Notes on sources:
1. Breytenbach, *Die Geskiedenis van die Tweede Vryheidsoorlog* Vol I p268.
2. Breytenbach, *Die Geskiedenis van die Tweede Vryheidsoorlog* Vol I p269.
3. Breytenbach, *Die Geskiedenis van die Tweede Vryheidsoorlog* Vol I pp 270-271.
4. Breytenbach, *Die Geskiedenis van die Tweede Vryheidsoorlog* Vol I p276.
5. Breytenbach, *Die Geskiedenis van die Tweede Vryheidsoorlog* Vol I p277.
6. Breytenbach, *Die Geskiedenis van die Tweede Vryheidsoorlog* Vol I p285.
7. Breytenbach, *Die Geskiedenis van die Tweede Vryheidsoorlog* Vol I p286.
8. Breytenbach, *Die Geskiedenis van die Tweede Vryheidsoorlog* Vol I pp279.
9. Denys Reitz *Commando* pp31-32. No other reference has been found as to who this signaling party might have been – Reitz is the only one who mentions them.
10. J.F. Naudé *Veg en Vlug* p39. We are not told to what use Naudé put his "beautiful sabre."
11. Breytenbach, *Die Geskiedenis van die Tweede Vryheidsoorlog* Vol I p286.
12. Van Warmelo *On Commando* p16.
13. Breytenbach, *Die Geskiedenis van die Tweede Vryheidsoorlog* Vol I pp30-31 gives a list of the campaigns against African tribal groups from 1854 to 1898.
14. Schikkerling *Commando Courageous* p11.

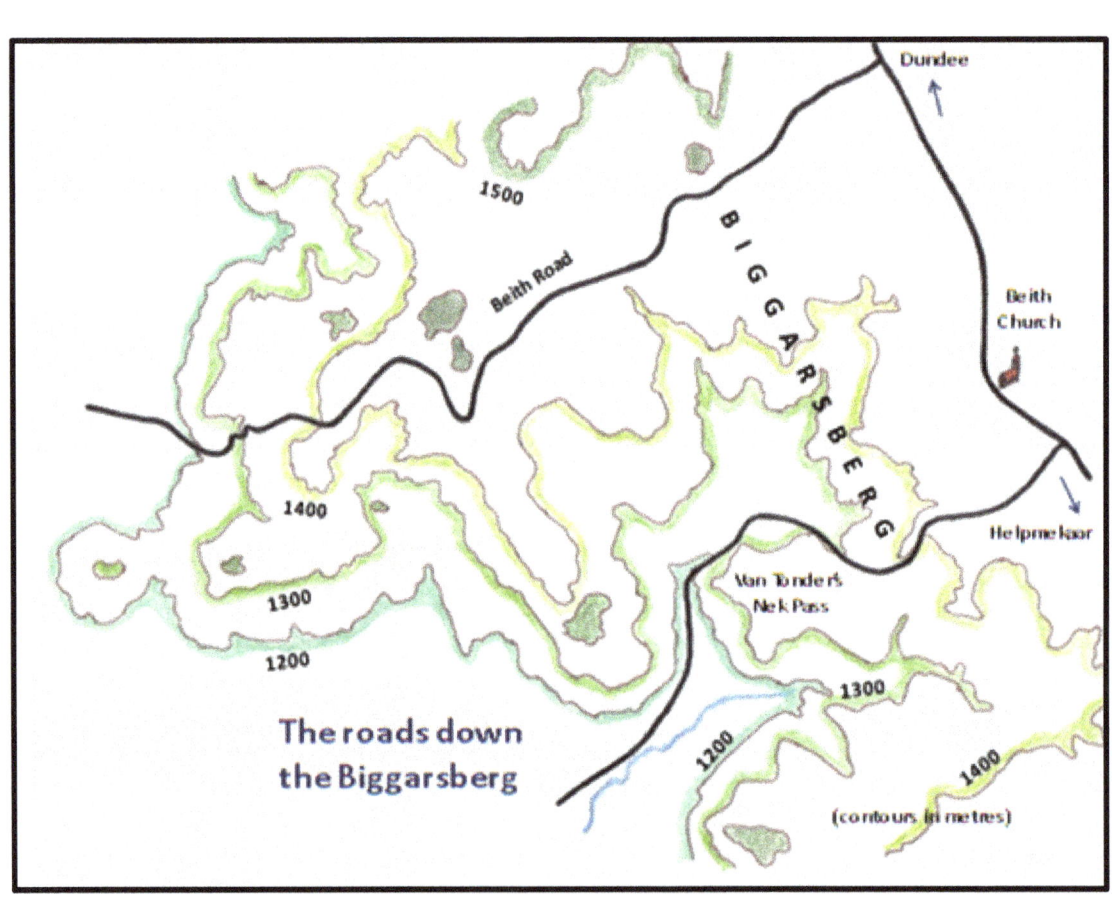

The roads down the Biggarsberg

The church at Beith.

Yule's column crossing a stream.
(from a photograph by George Lynch of the *Illustrated London News*)

Chapter 7

Across the Sundays River Valley
25 to 26 October 1899

"…the march was a very long one.
Indeed some think it beats Roberts' [march to Kandahar]"
(Gunner Netley's diary quoted in Pakenham, *The Boer War* p148)

The column made good time in daylight on Wednesday 25th October. The cavalry had had a hard day on Tuesday but the infantry had lain up along the bank of the Waschbank River and were somewhat rested by the time the march was resumed at 4 a.m. on Wednesday morning. Over the flat plains they were able to move with two or three wagons abreast which reduced the length of the column considerably and made it less vulnerable in the event of an attack. No Boers came near them even though the commando that Joubert had sent in pursuit and Meyer's scouting force must by then have set off after them. The sun shone, spirits rose and they all dried out a bit.

By 10 a.m. the Hussars advance guard had reached the Sundays River, crossed by a good drift, and halted about two miles further on to await the rest of the column and the baggage. Major Romer tells of the Dublins' march over this section, 'H' company having been marooned on the far side of the river by the sudden rush of water after the thunderstorm:

> At 5 a.m. on the 25th, in bright sunshine, the retreat was resumed. 'H' company crossed to the south bank a few minutes before the column moved off, although the water was still up to the men's waists. The Dublin Fusiliers formed the rearguard, and marched till midday, when Sundays River was reached. 'A' company remained on the north bank to cover the crossing of the waggons, and at 2.30 p.m. the column went on, only halting at 4.30 for tea. Everybody hoped to have a long rest here, but at 6.30 p.m. Major Bird was sent for, and informed that, as the Boers were in close pursuit, a night march was necessary. (Note 1)

Churcher and the Irish Fusiliers arrived at the camping ground at 3.45 p.m., "a nice piece of high ground covered with grass" where "we hoped to have a real good night's rest". Piquets were sent out, rations were distributed and cooked. Churcher took another photograph. The good night's rest was not to happen, however. Information had reached the 18th Hussars that the Boers had "just occupied the camp we were in the night before", information doubtless from the same source as the warning to the Dublin Fusiliers. At 4 p.m., around the time that this information was received, a patrol consisting of 'A' Squadron of the 5th Lancers arrived with orders from White to push on at once. Neither the Dublins nor the Irish Fusiliers seem to have been aware of the arrival of the Lancers, being at the rear of the column, even though the Lancers were "met with loud cheers from Yule's tired soldiers." (Note 2)

Somewhere around this time a newspaper correspondent, H.W. Nevinson, arrived. He had taken no small risk to get to there. He had been at Rietfontein, White's successful attempt to prevent the Free State army from interfering with the column, the day before. He had been in Bloemfontein and Pretoria a few days before war was declared. Then he had met Joubert on the train as he travelled to cross the frontier at Volksrust. He seems to have therefore concluded that there was no cause for concern that he might be interned in the very conceivable event that he would encounter the Boers. He left Ladysmith sometime on Wednesday morning and tells of his ride to meet the column:

> Next day I determined to meet the Dundee force on its way. They were reported to have halted about twenty-five miles off the night before, near Sundays River. About six miles out we had a small force ready to give them assistance if they were pursued. Passing through that column halted by a stream, I went on into more open country. For many miles I saw small parties of our Lancers and Carbineers scouring the country on both sides of the track.
>
> Then soon after I had crossed a wide watershed I came down into broken and rocky country again, well suited for Boers, and there the outposts ended. I had a wide view of distant mountains, far away to the Zulu border on the east, and northwards to the Biggarsberg and Dundee, a terrible country to cross with a retiring column, harassed by three days' fighting. The few white farmers had gone, of course, but, happily, I came across a Kaffir kraal, and a Kaffir chief himself came out to look at me. The Cape boy who was with me asked if he had seen any English troops that way. "Yes, there were many, many, many, hardly an hour's ride further on. He spoke the pretty Zulu language – it is something like Italian.

We went on. The track went steep downhill to a spruit where the water lay in pools. And there on the opposite hill was that gallant little British Army, halted in a position of extreme danger, absolutely commanded on all sides but one, and preparing for tea as unconcernedly as if they were in a Lockhart's shop in Goswell Road. (Note 3)

Now, instead of a rest, they had to push on. Whatever hardships and difficulties they had suffered up to now rather paled into insignificance compared to their march on Wednesday night. The ground over which they marched was soft loamy soil and, with rain falling in torrents, the track quickly became a morass. Romer describes the salutary experience suffered by the Dublins at the rear of the march:

> The brigade accordingly started at 7 p.m., at the same moment that heavy rain began to fall. The road quickly became inches deep in mud, everyone was soon wet to the skin, and the night was so dark that a man in each section of fours had to hold on to the canteen strap of the man in front in order to keep the proper direction. (Note 4)

Churcher had a similar experience:

> We fell in at 6 p.m., and had hardly started, before down came the rain in torrents. We were the main body of the rear guard and so just in rear of the baggage, the result being that the road, soon becoming well-nigh impassable for waggons, became blocked, and before we had gone a mile from camp we were stopped and kept three hours standing in the mud and pouring rain, the men not having either blankets or overcoats. The whole night long it rained, and the whole night we crawled along, perhaps doing on average about half-a-mile an hour. It was pitch dark, and altogether it was the most poisonously miserable night that any man could or will ever experience. (Note 5)

Gunner Netley, however, seemed not downhearted, this cheerfulness under extremely trying circumstances being characteristic of the British soldier:

> The General came in with an escort of lancers and told us that his force was…8 miles further ahead, and of course that bucked us up a bit. He left orders for us to join him, so we moved off amid a drenching rain, and we had not got far before the column was reported broken (in two), which meant another hour's wait in the Natal April shower. It was also very dark, and what with the roads being about 6 inches deep in mud, it is beautiful. We can't move along sharp because the wagons, which would if not taken in hand properly, probably fall into a donga [ravine] and then something would happen you could bet. At 12 midnight that April shower is still showering and the drenched column is sticking it like Britons … (Note 6)

George Steevens, correspondent of the *Daily Mail*, and a man who had been at Omdurman in the Sudan in 1898, had also ridden out to the column. He decided that it was:

> no use waiting for sensational stories among these men. No use waiting for fighting either; in open country the force could have knocked thousands of Boers to pieces, and there was not the least chance of the Boers coming to be knocked. So I rode back through the rolling veldt basin.

He evidently made it back into Ladysmith before the storm struck:

> Coming through I noticed that the sky over Ladysmith was very black. The great inky stain of cloud spread and ran up the heavens, then down to the whole circumference. In five minutes it was night and rain-storm. It stung like a whiplash; to meet it was like riding into a wall. Ladysmith streets were ankle deep in half an hour; the camps were morass and pond. And listening to the ever-fresh bursts hammering all evening on to deepening pools, we learned that the Dundee men had not camped after all, had marched at six, and were coming on all night into Ladysmith. Thirty-two miles without rest, through stinging cataract and spongy loam and glassy slime! (Note 7)

Lieutenant W.T. Willcox of the 5th Lancers also tells of this awful night, though certainly not from first hand:

> This last march of the retiring column was a frightful ordeal to the hungry and weary soldiers from Dundee; streaming torrents of rain all night, and inches of mud to toil through. Oxen and horses fell in their traces and were left to die. It sometimes took hours to cover a hundred yards. However, the men and animals crawled steadily on through mud and rain, and at daybreak reached the Modder Spruit, where the remainder of the 5th Lancers were in bivouac awaiting them. From here a short march brought the Column into Ladysmith. (Note 8)

Things were not that simple. White had, as promised to Yule, sent out a force to meet him of which the 5th Lancers were the advance guard. Part of this force was the Natal Carbineers. Trooper Shaw had been actively engaged at Rietfontein on 24th October. He tells of his experiences the following day when they went out along the Helpmekaar road:

> The next morning, that of 25th October, we expected to pass in peace, but at about ten o'clock orders came round that we were to parade with "stripped" saddles; no blankets or rations were to be carried. We were to make a short march out of Town to complimentarily bring in General Yule's Column. At midday we had the pleasure of seeing a large herd of Hartebeeste – they were of course preserved. The enemy afterwards exterminated them. We continued our march and my squadron eventually found itself at about four o'clock posted in a defile through which ran the high road. General Yule's column was reported to be some five miles further ahead. It was quite evident that our complimentary ride was going to cost us a miserable night out for heavy black thunder clouds were banking up in the Drakensberg. We were posted on the right of the defile, some of the Border Mounted Rifles held the left, and a Cossack Post of three men crouched under a stone wall which ran by the side of the road below us. In an hour the storm broke and I was very glad of the heavy cloak that despite orders I had brought with me. The rain came down in sheets and the blackness of the night soon made it impossible to see a foot before one. I can hardly remember such a pitchy black night before or since and as I was becoming decidedly hungry I was absolutely disgusted when I was one of the unfortunates chosen to form a Cossack Post further along the gorge. We slipped and scrambled and tumbled along and were eventually "posted". Sometime before midnight the sky cleared a little and we heard the tramp of men in the road below us – the advance guard of Yule's column. A mule broke loose and caused a small panic among some of the men. They flung themselves over the low wall, rifles, helmets, and men falling in all directions, and in the confusion swarmed the Cossack Post stationed there. The slouch hats inspired them with the idea that the men of the post were Boers and they at once were for killing off the unfortunate troopers. A match was eventually struck in the shelter of a smasher-hat and the silver buttons being exhibited the Yule's men were pacified. Having been given their helmets they returned to the road. The stream of men was now constant and we soon heard the rumble of gun-wheels. The tramping and rumbling toned down by the swish of the rain continued for what seemed an interminable time but at last we were ordered to re-join the squadron and march. Then followed a long wearisome toil after a guide with a lantern; sometimes we were on the road and sometimes off. I nearly fell asleep on my horse and had just reduced myself to a state of mental torpor when the Column halted. We dismoun-ted in a sea of mud, whipped by a blinding rain, and lying down at my horse's head I quickly fell asleep. (Note 9)

Things clearly became very confused in the dark night and both Churcher and Romer tell of some confusion as to the right road. First Churcher, his entry for 26th October:

> At dawn this morning we found ourselves quite alone, but luckily on the main road, so we halted at a farmhouse and collected the stragglers, which considering all things, were very few. After halting for an hour we continued our march, and four miles further on we found a small force waiting for us at Modder Spruit with food and water. Here we breakfasted, and the men had tea, and at 10 a.m. continued our march another nine miles into Ladysmith, arriving at our camp there about 1 p.m. (Note 10)

Major Romer's men had had just as difficult a march as the rest and especially as they were the rearguard. At dawn the next morning they found the battalion to be "luckily in its proper place behind the column, and without a man missing." The Dublins arrived at the Modder River at 8 a.m., covering only eleven miles in the last twelve hours.

Netley suggests that the column split into two and took different roads into Ladysmith. Study of a contemporary map of Ladysmith and the surrounding roads and tracks seems to confirm that this might well have happened. He continued with:

> ...and at 4 a.m. we passed the other column in camp, thank God. It would have done your eye good to see the difference in Tommy that morning, and see the same man at home... Worn out, wet through, covered in mud from head to foot... A Kodak would have been useful on the scene then especially when the drying clothes business came off. Fancy taking off everything and while it is drying to keep yourself to yourself by running around like a Kaffir. (sic) When the clothes were on again, we proceeded again with the column towards Ladysmith and reached it all correct, properly worn out... the march was a very long one. Indeed some people think it beats Roberts' [march to Kandahar]. (Note 11)

By early afternoon the entire force had arrived in Ladysmith. There were no human casualties on the march although Yule was apparently was "almost prostrate with illness and fatigue." Apart from the Lancers, no one mentions any animal casualties although it is likely that numbers of them failed to make it into Ladysmith. Cavalrymen would naturally be more sympathetic and caring of their animals. The fugitives were greeted with some enthusiasm by the garrison in Ladysmith – the Manchesters, Gloucesters and Devons all did their bit in helping to make them comfortable. Churcher said that "The Manchester Regiment in a most kind and thoughtful manner, provided both officers and men with an excellent lunch." The Dublins were provided for by the Devonshire and Gloucestershire Regiments in like manner. Sleep was needed even more than food – Major Bird, the acting CO of the Dublins was seen to be asleep in the saddle as he rode into town to report personally to General White. (Note 12)

There was to be little chance for rest however as Ian Hamilton had proposed an attack on the approaching Boers on 27th October and some of the Dundee men were to be involved. A good meal, overnight's rest and receipt of letters from home cheered them up a good deal and they were ready for action the next morning.

Notes on sources:
1. Romer and Mainwaring *The Second Battalion Royal Dublin Fusiliers in the South African War* p20. Nothing is said about the 18th Hussars patrol also cut off for a while by the torrent so we must presume that the mounted men easily crossed the flooded stream.
2. Burnett, *The 18th Hussars in South Africa* p44. No source is given for this piece of information (that the Boers had "just occupied the camp we were in the night before.") but it was likely to have been a local Zulu. Certainly it is possible that the one hundred men from Meyer's force, as well as the commando of five hundred sent by Joubert, had reached the bivouac site on the Waschbank River occupied by Yule the previous night. Willcox *The Fifth (Royal Irish) Lancers in South Africa* p223 says the patrol met the column at the Sundays River. It is clear that the column was in fact some way past the Sundays River when the Lancers encountered them.
3. Nevinson *The Diary of a Siege* pp47-48. Nevinson could not have left Ladysmith much before 11 a.m. as he seems only to have encountered the column at about 4 p.m. How he actually obtained intelligence of the column's whereabouts does not seem to be explained. Nevinson later became an activist for the enfranchisement of women. In South Africa he was employed by the *Daily Chronicle* but wrote for many years for the *Manchester Guardian*. He reported on a number of wars and was wounded at Gallipoli.
4. Romer and Mainwaring *The Second Battalion Royal Dublin Fusiliers in the South African War* p20.
5. Churcher *With the Irish Fusiliers from Alexandria to Natal* p26.
6. Gunner Netley's diary quoted in Pakenham, *The Boer War* p148.
7. Steevens *From Cape Town to Ladysmith* pp69-70. Steevens died soon after Christmas 1899 of typhoid fever and is buried in Ladysmith Town cemetery.
8. Willcox *The Fifth (Royal Irish) Lancers in South Africa* p223.
9. Shaw *Trooper* pp35-36.
10. Churcher *With the Irish Fusiliers from Alexandria to Natal* p26.
11. Gunner Netley's diary quoted in Pakenham, *The Boer War* p148.
12. From Major Bird's unpublished diary.

The last few miles:
The column approaches Ladysmith.
– one of Major Churcher's pictures (above)

Entering the town.

Both pictures from the morning of 26th October 1899.

The Leicesters reach Ladysmith – sometime on Thursday, 26th October 1899.

Chapter 8

Safe in Ladysmith
26 October 1899 and afterwards

"…all through the whole force had behaved splendidly."
(An officer of the 18th Hussars)

Commandant General Piet Joubert had advanced the Transvaal army's headquarters to Glencoe and at 10.15 p.m. on 25th October, there he received an indignant telegram from the Chief Commandant of the Orange Free State Marthinus Prinsloo: (translated from the Dutch)

> I deeply regret that your men have not yet arrived after I sent you a message yesterday that the troops from Ladysmith had advanced on my position and I had found it impossible to send reinforcements from here. If your burgers do not arrive soon, I will order my burgers to vacate their position. (Note 1)

Prinsloo, had been hauled over the coals by his President, Marthinus Steyn, for not providing assistance for the Transvaalers at Elandslaagte, but was now complaining in turn that Joubert was not now supporting him. President Kruger had been in telegraphic contact with Steyn over the Elandslaagte matter, and now was involving himself once more. A copy of Prinsloo's telegram had been sent to him and he sent back to Joubert, asking him just where the Transvaal commandos were and why they had not yet joined up with the Free State men. An embarrassed Piet Joubert, Kruger's political opponent, the two men being not exactly the best of friends, could only respond that he had ordered Colonel Trichardt and General Erasmus to immediately advance and combine with the Free Staters at the Modder Spruit. Advanced Boer units were in the vicinity of Waschbank on the evening of 25th October but they were delayed by "rain that was falling so hard that nothing could be made out" – the same rainstorm that caused such suffering to Yule and his men. It was only on the afternoon of 26th October that the first Transvaal forces arrived at Elandslaagte and made contact with the Free Staters. It was another two days, Saturday 28th October before all the Boer forces had closed up around Ladysmith.

Far from mounting a vigorous pursuit, Joubert was consumed with the irrational fear that Yule, reinforced by some of White's men from Ladysmith, was about to mount a counter-attack. Yule's force of 4,000 soldiers, cavalry, artillery and infantry was safe once they had descended the Biggarsberg provided that they kept moving. The Boers did not even mount raids to harry the rearguard. At that stage of the war what would later become their principal advantage over the British – superior mobility – had not been recognized and utilized. Nor had younger and more vigorous generals succeeded to the command of the Boer forces who could utilize this advantage.

The Natal Carbineers had returned to Ladysmith with the rearguard of Yule's column but one squadron was given the task of climbing Bulwana mountain. Trooper Shaw was hungry and a little disheveled, no doubt, and climbing up the steep slope was not to his liking but he seems to have spent a fairly uneventful day, 26th October, on the summit:

> Early next morning we woke and welcomed a hot sun that very soon set our camping ground steaming and sent our spirits bounding up. The road not far from where we had dismounted was alive with mud-covered, tired men of the 60th Rifles, Dublin Fusiliers, 18th Hussars, Leicesters and others. Waggons and water carts passed by, others stuck fast in the deep loamy soil, field guns with their limbers laboured through the rushing stream at our feet. The road itself was in a fearful condition; naturally loose soil, the rain combined with the passage over it of thousands of men with impedimenta had reduced it to a veritable "slough of despond". It was a miserable yet impressive sight. An hour or two later a couple of squadron mule waggons arrived from Ladysmith with some biscuits and coffee and horse feed for other squadrons than my own. Our squadron instead received orders to fall back upon the "Nek" of Lombard's Kop and later to climb and take up a position on the huge Umbulwana Mountain.
>
> Upon this mountain we spent the rest of the day. I walked over most of the plateau and from the shade of the loose-barked "Cabbage tree" under which I spent most of my day's vigil, could be seen the concentrating forces of the enemy. Each of the three laagers was sheltered under the aegis of a huge red-cross flag that would fitfully extend in the breeze. At about four o'clock that evening the squadron received orders to march into Town. Thoroughly glad we were to see once more the Squadron Quartermaster-Sergeant's tent. (Note 2)

White was still not resigned to being shut up and besieged in Ladysmith. The major problem was that it was an unhealthy place, where typhoid and enteric fever were rife even in peacetime. The water supply was not secure since the Boers controlled the Klip River upstream of the town and could, and indeed would, poison this supply. The first to die from drinking the water were three cavalry horses. The British found this tactic to be distinctly unsporting. Wars that the British army had waged up until then were decided with one major battle which would determine the issue. White hoped that he could destroy the Boer army before the town was surrounded. Ian Hamilton's scouts had seen an unprotected Boer laager to the east of the town and obtained permission from White to launch an attack on it on Friday 27th October. With this in mind Hamilton took out his brigade, of which Major Churcher and the Royal Irish Fusiliers were now a part, to Modderspruit that morning:

> We got to Modder Spruit at about one o'clock, where we halted, and General Hamilton asked all the officers to the top of the ridge to see the situation. The Boers' scouts were plainly visible about 5,000 yards off. Presently Sir George White arrived, and we had orders to bivouac for the present, but at 8 o'clock they issued orders, and these were that the Boer position was to be assaulted with the bayonet at daybreak, the Royal Irish Fusiliers to lead. The Colonel gave G Company the post of honour at the front, and we all lay down for a little rest before advancing at 2 a.m. However, they must have changed their minds, for about 12-30 orders came round that plans had been changed, and that we were to start to march back to Ladysmith at 3-15 a.m. (Note 3)

Churcher's diary continues for Saturday 28th October:

> I do hope we shall be left in peace today, for the men want a wash and a clean up badly, and so do all of us, but our orders are to be ready to fall in at a moment's notice. All sorts of shaves are flying about town, and everyone is in a very jumpy state. They got a war balloon here today, and are filling it, so we shall be safe from surprise. They are also bringing two heavy guns from Durban with a naval contingent, but we hear that the Boers have cut our water supply, which is a nuisance. I dined at the Royal Hotel in the evening, it was crammed with all sorts and conditions of men, war correspondents at one table with Melton Prior at the head, members of the Volunteer Corps and refugees from Johannesburg. Got back to camp at 9 and found the Mess Tent full of orders and counter orders, and up to 12 o'clock orderlies came dropping in at intervals. After which there was peace and we managed to get our well-earned sleep. (Note 4)

Hamilton's proposed attack on the Boer laager had been cancelled at the last minute by Sir George White who had a much bigger attack in mind. The Governor of Natal, Sir Walter Hely-Hutchinson, was greatly concerned that Pietermaritzburg and Durban were defenceless with only a handful of troops in each place. By way of reassurance, White telegraphed that he had located a "sufficiently large force of the enemy with guns to make a good objective" and that an attack would take place next morning. On Monday, 30th October the attack duly took place. Yule was ill and on his way back to hospital in Durban. His Dundee brigade was commanded by Colonel Geoffrey Grimwood but Churcher was ill and ordered to remain in camp, "which is a bitter disappointment."

Grimwood was unable to press home an attack against an enemy that was invisible and not where it was supposed to be. Nearly one thousand prisoners were taken by the Boers at Nicholson's Nek while the Leicesters and the 60th Rifles, still not fully recovered from their long march, were forced back into Ladysmith, tired and thirsty once again. This was "Mournful Monday" and the worst humiliation that the British army had suffered in many years. Two days later the Boers cut the railway line south of Ladysmith and the telegraph line to Pietermaritzburg went dead. Ladysmith was surrounded.

Whatever may be said about Penn Symons and his hopelessly unrealistic view of the defence of the Colony of Natal and the town of Dundee in particular, his action at Talana brought the Boers' already slow advance to a halt for several days. This delay was critical in that it allowed the Royal Navy to bring into Ladysmith a number of heavy naval guns that were certainly crucial to the defence. Yule's successful retirement back to Ladysmith considerably enlarged the force, cavalry, artillery and infantry, that White now had under his command to defend the town. Until the setback of 30th October he evidently did not expect to be surrounded and besieged in Ladysmith. After this, he now had no alternative but to sit tight and await relief from the south. It would be four long months before Buller's advance guard galloped into town as the Boers retreated back over the Biggarsberg.

Notes on sources:
1. Breytenbach, *Die Geskiedenis van die Tweede Vryheidsoorlog* Vol I p301.
2. Shaw *Trooper* p36-37.
3. Churcher *With the Irish Fusiliers from Alexandria to Natal* p27.
4. Churcher *With the Irish Fusiliers from Alexandria to Natal* pp27-28.

Kommando of korps	Aantal dienspligtige manskappe	Getal aan front aanwesig op 11 Okt. '99	Persentasie aan front
Bethal	781	400 w.o. 360 berede	51·2
Ermelo	862	580 ,, 400 ,,	67·3
Heidelberg	1,578	1,211 ,, 946 ,,	76·7
Krugersdorp	900	860 ,, 650 ,,	95·5
Middelburg	2,081	769	36·9
Pretoria	3,746	1,492 ,, 1,072 ,,	39·8
Standerton	1,130	657 ,, 555 ,,	58·1
Wakkerstroom	1,254	713 ,, 670 ,,	56·8
Utrecht	775		
Vryheid	944	1,720	80·0
Piet Retief	432		
Staatsartillerie		320 ,, 320 ,,	
Hollanderkorps		152 ,, 119 ,,	
Duitse korps			
Ierse korps		2,508	
Goudvelde (Witwatersrand)			
Totaal		11,382	

APPENDIX 4.

STRENGTH OF BURGHER ARMY OF SOUTH AFRICAN REPUBLIC.

District.	Present on Mobilisation.	Subsequent Increase.
Bethel	700	
Bloemhof	800	
Carolina	506	
Ermelo	800	
Fordsburg	900	
Germiston and Boksburg	1,050	
Heidelberg	1,685	
Jeppestown	400	
Johannesburg*	1,000	
Krugersdorp	800	
Lichtenburg	850	
Lydenburg	1,230	
Marico	1,050	14,779 ‡
Middelburg	1,317	
Piet Retief	230	
Potchefstroom	3,000	
Pretoria	2,540	
Rustenburg	1,500	
Springs	60	
Standerton	1,100	
Swaziland*	290	
Utrecht	900	
Vryheid	944	
Waterberg	732	
Wakkerstroom	800	
Wolmaranstad	400	
Zoutpansberg	1,287	
	26,871†	14,779

Total Transvaal Burghers in the field ... 41,650

* Exclusive of police. † Boer evidence. ‡ Intelligence statistics on conclusion of peace.

APPENDIX 3.

The distribution of British forces under arms in Natal on 11th October, 1899.

DUNDEE*	18th Hussars. One sqdn., Natal Carbineers. M.I. coy., 1st battn. Leicestershire regiment. M.I. coy., 1st battn. King's Royal Rifle Corps. M.I. coy., 2nd battn. Royal Dublin Fusiliers. Detachment Natal Police. 13th, 67th, and 69th batteries, R.F.A. 1st battn. Leicestershire regt. 1st battn. King's Royal Rifle Corps. 2nd battn. Royal Dublin Fusiliers.
LADYSMITH	5th Lancers. 19th Hussars. 21st, 42nd, and 53rd batteries, R.F.A. 10th mountain battery, R.G.A. 23rd coy., R.E. 1st battn. Liverpool regt. and M.I. coy. 1st battn. Devonshire regt. 1st battn. Manchester regt. 2nd battn. Gordon Highlanders. Natal Mounted Rifles. Natal Carbineers. Border Mounted Rifles. Natal Field artillery. Detachment Natal Police. Natal Naval Volunteers. Natal Corps of Guides.
COLENSO	Durban Light Infantry. Detachment Natal Naval Volunteers. One sqdn., Natal Carbineers.
ESTCOURT	Natal Royal Rifles.
PIETERMARITZBURG	2nd battn. King's Royal Rifle Corps. Imperial Light Horse.
HELPMAKAAR	Umvoti Mounted Rifles.
ESHOWE	One mounted coy., 1st battn. King's Royal Rifle Corps.
DURBAN	One sqdn., 5th Dragoon Guards.

* The 1st battn. Royal Irish Fusiliers, and one section, 23rd coy., R.E., arrived at Dundee during 15th and 16th October.

From Maurice – the Official History.

The tables above give the Boer strength at Talana (Breytenbach) and the strength on the outbreak of war and the subsequent increase (Maurice – the Official History).

Bibliography

Published documents: Books and articles.
1. L.S. Amery, *The Times History of the war in South Africa* Vol II Sampson, Low, Marston and Company, Ltd London 1905.
2. The Marquess of Anglesey *A History of the British Cavalry Volume IV 1899-1913* Leo Cooper, London 1986.
3. Michael Asher *Khartoum – the Ultimate Imperial Adventure* Viking, London 2005.
4. Gerard Bailey *Seven months under Boer rule* R.A. Burns and Co, Dundee 1999.
5. J.H. Breytenbach, *Die Geskiedenis van die Tweede Vryheidsoorlog in Suid-Afrika, 1899 – 1902* Vol I State Printer, Pretoria 1986.
6. Major Charles Burnett *The 18th Hussars in South Africa* Warren & Son, Winchester 1905.
7. Lieutenant General Sir William Butler *An Autobiography* Charles Scribner's Sons, New York 1911.
8. Ruari Chisholm, *Ladysmith* Jonathan Ball Publishers, Johannesburg 1979.
9. Major D.C. Churcher *With the Irish Fusiliers from Alexandria to Natal 1899 – 1900.* Boer War Books, York 1984.
10. Louis Creswicke *South Africa and the Transvaal War* Vol II T.C. & E.C. Jack, Edinburgh 1900.
11. Lionel Crook *Artillery of the Anglo-Boer War 1899 – 1902*, Kraal Publishers, Brandfort 2003.
12. Christiaan de Wet *Three Years' War*, 1903
13. Sir Mortimer Durand *The Life of Field-Marshal Sir George White* Volume II William Blackwood and Sons, Edinburgh and London 1915.
14. John Gooch, *The Boer War* Routledge, London 2000.
15. Archie Hunter *Kitchener's Sword Arm* Sarpedon, New York 1996.
16. Major General Sir Frederick Maurice, *History of the war in South Africa* (the Official History) Hurst and Blackett Limited, London 1908 (reprint Naval & Military Press).
17. Edited by Major General Sir Frederick Maurice *Soldier, Artist, Sportsman – The Life of General Lord Rawlinson of Trent* Houghton Mifflin Company, New York 1928.
18. J.F. Naudé *Veg en Vlug* Nijgh & Van Dittmar, Rotterdam 1904 (reprint Bienedell Uitgewers, Pretoria 1998.)
19. H.W. Nevinson *The Diary of a Siege* Methuen & Co., London 1900.
20. Thomas Pakenham, *The Boer War* Weidenfeld and Nicholson Limited, 1979.
21. H.J.C. Pieterse *Oorlogsavonture van Genl. Wynand Malan* Nasionale Pers Beperk, Cape Town 1946.
22. Fransjohan Pretorius *Life on Commando during the Anglo-Boer War 1899-1902.* Human & Rousseau, Cape Town, Pretoria, Johannesburg 1999. An English translation of an original Afrikaans work.
23. Denys Reitz *Commando* Faber and Faber Limited, London 1929 (reprint 1983).
24. Major C.F. Romer and Major A.E. Mainwaring *The Second Battalion Royal Dublin Fusiliers in the South African War* A.L. Humphreys, London 1908.
25. R.W. Schikkerling *Commando Courageous* Hugh Keartland (Publishers), Johannesburg 1964.
26. Iain R. Smith *The Origins of the South African War 1899-1902* Longman, Harlow 1996.
27. Spink auction catalogue *The Anglo-Boer War Anniversary 1899-1999 – Orders, Decorations and Campaign Medals.* Spink & Son Ltd, London 1999.
28. G.W. Steevens *From Cape Town to Ladysmith* The Copp Clark Co., Limited, Toronto 1900.
29. Ian Uys *Heidelbergers of the Boer War* Ian Uys, Rensburg 1981.
30. Dietlof van Warmelo *On Commando* A.D. Jonker/Publisher, Johannesburg 1977.
31. Major W.T. Willcox *The Fifth (Royal Irish) Lancers in South Africa 1899 – 1902* Boer War Books, York 1981.

Primary source documents: Diaries, newspapers.
1. Lieutenant C.T.W. Grimshaw My experiences in the Boer War (1899-1900). Transcribed from an unpublished account of an officer in the 2nd Battalion Dublin Fusiliers.
2. Trooper Dacre Shaw, Natal Carbineers, Trooper, privately printed.
3. Pen Pictures of the War by Men at the Front. London 1900.

Index

5th Lancers	28,44,45,47
18th Field Hospital	35
18th Hussars	19,21,23,24,28-30,35-37,44,49
60th Rifles	21,24,49,50
Adelaide Farm	24
Altham, E.A.	22
Amery, Leo	20
Anglo-Zulu War	6,7
Bailey, Gerard (Rev)	21,24,30,34,35,39
Baldry, James	30,39
Beith	36,38,43
Bell's Kop	15
Bethel	15
Biggarsberg	6,14,16,19,20,29,36,40,44,49,50
Bird, Major	44,47
Blesboklaagte	35
Bloemfontein	44
Boksburg	13,22,29
Border Mounted Rifles	46
Botha, Louis	15,17,41
Breijtenbach	16
Brenman, Pte	23
Buffalo River	6,13,16,20-22
Buller, Redvers	7,9,50
Bulwana	49
Burger, Schalk	15,16,39,41
Burnett, Major	35
Butler, William	6,9,12
Cape Town	7
Carleton, G.D.	28
Carleton, F.R.C.	24,28
Chamberlain, Joseph	6
Charleston	14
Chisholm, John Scott	30
Churcher, D.W.	22,28,29,34,36,37,44-48,50
Clarke, Lieutenant	36
Clegg, Private	30
Conyngham-Greene, William	8,12
Cox, George	6
Dannhauser	14-17,20,22,28,29
Dartnell, John	29,31,33,34,37
Davey, Captain	21
Decker's Farm	31
De Jager's Drift	15,16,22
Derckse, Field Cornet	14,15,22
Devonshire Regiment	24,47
Dewaas	35
De Wet, Christiaan	30
Donegan, Major	35,40
Doringberg (Dooneberg)	15,16,23
Dragoon Guards	9,28
Duff, Beauchamp	8
Dundee	5,7-10,14-17,20-22,25,28-31,33,35,39-41,44,45,47,50
Durant, Mortimer	20
Durban	7,8,29,50
East London	7
Elandslaagte	16,22,28-31,33,37,39,40,49
Erasmus, D.J.E. "Maroela"/Maroola	13-17,24,39-41,49
Ermelo	16
Escombe, Harry	11,31,33
Eshowe	16
Esterhuizen, Field Cornet	14
Faulkner	22
French, John	28,33
German Corps	14
Germiston	13-15,30
Glencoe	8,9,16,20,22,29-31,34,39,41,49
Glencoe Field Force	5,6,21,25,31,34,39
Gloucester Regiment	9,47
Goodenough, W.H.	6
Grahamstown	6
Greytown	5,29,31,34,35,40
Grimshaw, Cecil T.W.	16,22-24
Grimwood, Geoffrey	50
Grobbler, Hans	16
Guilfoyle, Sergeant	23
Gunning, Robert	24,25
Hamilton, Ian	7,8,28,31,47,50
Hannah, W.M.J.	28
Hattinghspruit / Hatting	16,20,28,39,40
Heidelberg	13,16,22,29,30
Helpmekaar	22,29-31,33,41,46
Hely-Hutchinson, Walter	8,12,50
Hime, Albert	11,20
Hollander Corps	14
Hunter, Archibald	7,8,28
Imbabane Hills	15
Indumene	29,40
Impati	17,20,21,24,28,29,34-36,39,40
Ingogo River	14
Jameson, Leander Starr	6,39
Johannesburg	6,7,14,16,37,39,50
Joubert, Piet	9,13,14,17,22,28,39-41,44,47,49
King's Royal Rifles	21,22
Kitchener, Herbert	25
Klip river	50
Kock, Jan	14,16,28,29,39,41
Kruger, Caspar	17
Kruger, Paul	6,7,13,17,39,49
Krugersdorp	15,16

Ladysmith......5,6,8,9,14,16,22,28-31,33-35,37-41,44-50	Ryley, Mr. 31
Laming, H.T. 30	Sandberg, Carl 7
Landman's Drift 16,22	Sandspruit 13,23
Landsdowne, Lord 7	Schiel, Adolf 14,16
Leicester Regiment 28,31,49,50	Shaw, Trooper 45,49
Lennox Hill 17,20	Schutte, Commandant 39
Lombard, J.P. la G. 14	Shewan, Lieutenant 36
Lombard's Kop 49	Simpson 22
Lonsdale, Captain 21	Smith's Farm/Hill/Nek 20,24,31
Magoeba, Chief 13	Smuts, Jan 14,40
Majuba 24	Snaith, F.C. 37
Malan, Wynand 14	SS *Scot*. 7
Manchester Regiment 47	Steevens, George 45,47n
Meyer, Lucas 6,14-17,22,24,35,39-41,44	Steyn, Martinus 7-9,20,39,49
Middelburg 15	Sundays River 5,30,44
Milner, Alfred 6,7,12	Swaziland 15,16,39
Modder River/Spruit 37,45,46,49,50	Symons, William Penn 5,7-9,12,20-25,28,29,31,34,50
Möller, B.D. 24,25	Talana 5,16,17,20,23,24,28-31,34,40,41,50,51
Mulamgeni Mountains 23	Tongoland 16
Murray, A.J. 22	Trichardt, S.P.E. 16,24,35,39-41,49
Murray, Father 34	Tugela 6-9
Natal Carbineers 9,35,44,45,49	Utrecht 13,15,16
Natal Mounted Police 6,14,15,21,29	Vallentin, John 9
Natal Volunteers 20	Van Tonder's Nek 5,36
Naudé, J.F. 13-15,30,33,41	Vant's Drift (Barrt's) 16,22
Netley, William 34,45,46	Van Warmelo, Dietlof 41
Nevinson, H.W. 44,47	Van Wyk, Naas 14
Nicholson's Nek 50	Viljoen, Ben 16,39
Newcastle 6,8,14,20,21	Vlakfontein 36
Nottingham Road 9	Volksrust 13,44
Padwick, Corporal 30	Vrede 15
Paris, H.H. 29,35	Vryheid 13,15-17,36
Pienaar, Field Cornet 14,22	Wakkerstroom 15,16
Pietermaritzburg 5,8,22,29,50	Walker, W.H.F. Forestier 7
Piet Retief 13	Waschbank River 5,16,22,30,36,39,44,47,49
Potgieter, Field Cornet 16	Weilbach, J.D. 15,16,22,29,30,39-41
Potgieter farm 36	Wessels Nek 36,37
Pretoria 8,13,15,16,24,30,39,44	White, George ... 5-9,12,16,20-22,28,29,31,33-38,44,45, 47,49,50
Pretorius 39	Wickham, Major 31
Prince Imperial 21	Willcox, W.T. 45
Prinsloo, Marthinus 40,49	Willson, Charlie 35,37
Prior, Melton 50	Wolseley, Garnet 6,7
Rawlinson, Henry 7-10,28	Wools Drift 13
Reitz, Denys 13,17	Yule, James 5,12,24,25,28-31,33,35-41,44-47,49,50
Reitz, Francis 8,13	
Rhodes, Cecil John 6	
Rietfontein 30,33,38,44,45	
Roberts, Frederick 47	
Robinson, Mr. 23	
Romer, C.F. 36,44-46	
Royal Dublin Fusiliers ... 16,19,21,23,24,34,36,44-47,49	
Royal Field Artillery (R.F.A.) 31,34,36	
Royal Irish Fusiliers 22,24,28,36,44,50	
Royal Irish Rifles 9	
Royal Navy 50	

www.ingramcontent.com/pod-product-compliance
Lightning Source LLC
Chambersburg PA
CBHW040044090426
42734CB00024B/3490